COMPENDIUM

Spiritual Care through Muslim Ethnographic Stories

Harvard vs SubhanAllah

Volume 3

Dr. Yunus Kumek

Sage Chronicle ^λ
publishing house

Cover image: Unsplash.com

Sage Chronicle $^{\lambda}$
publishing house

www.sagechronicle.org
3380 Sheridan Drive, #240
New York 14226
contact@sagechronicle.org

ISBN 978-1-951050-23-8

Published in the United States of America.

PREFACE

This book brings into our contemporary life important Muslim teachings in a one-page story format. Each story has the first paragraph as the story and the second paragraph as the meanings and interpretations of the practice. The stories in the book aim to use contemporary life encounters with the meanings and interpretations in Islamic practice. These stories have been compiled and contemporized from ethnographic field work in different Sufi communities of New York, Boston, Pittsburgh, Chicago, Toronto, Istanbul, and Cairo.

The book uses a simple transliteration scheme from the original language of Arabic without going to the details of academic transliteration scheme. When there are names or referrals to God then the words are capitalized such as the Divine. The abbreviation used for the Prophet Muhammad is the Prophet. The footnotes with numbered superscripts give the immediate relevant information for the unfamiliar English reader. The endnotes with lettered superscripts give the information for the reader who is familiar with the teachings and readings in Sufism. The references with numbered and parenthesis superscripts allude to the notions in practice as some examples of these practices in the literature. The suggested readings are examples of some classical and contemporary work about the topic for interested readers. The glossary and index in the book can hopefully make it easier for general readers of English.

The short stories and anecdotes in this book can bring important and practical aspects of these teachings in our practical life. This book can be valuable for different level readers such as the Muslims, Christians, Jews, Buddhists, Hindus, and people who especially value spirituality and experiential knowledge and believe the mysteries of life beyond the seen and human control. Regardless of different naming of the deity as Allah, God, Adonai, or the notions of Nirvana or Samadhi, in this book, one can realize the similarity of common and intersecting points of spirituality or religious experience among different traditions.

The word "Sufi" or character of "Sufi" does not imply a group or sect in this case, but used to depict a self-reflective personality or a character trying to have a spiritual Muslim care in daily practices. So, each time you see the Sufi character, you can imagine and replace it with a "Muslim". It was also easy for me especially for Western audience just to denote everything as one character as Muslim without changing genders and trying to find 500 different Muslim gender names in more than 500 stories.

This book can be a valuable supplementary text in the disciplines of psychology, counseling, anthropology, philosophy, and religion.

Yunus Kumek, PhD
Lecturer in Muslim Ministry
Harvard Divinity School
Fall 2022

CONTENTS

COMPENDIUM

Spiritual Care through Muslim Ethnographic Stories

Harvard vs SubhanAllah

1.   Intentions for Food and Fun

One day, the Sufi was thinking, "I eat every day. I want to have fun every day. How can I make these times valuable for Allah ﷻ as well as similar to my prayers and worship?" She kept thinking and thinking until finally she exclaimed, "*Alhamdulillah*, thanks to Allah ﷻ, it is my intention."

In practice

Intention is the key for everything.[28] There are permissible things in religion such as eating and having fun. A person can turn those permissible things into worship if she or he makes an intention saying, "I am eating so that I can worship better. I am giving break to worship or prayer by having some fun so that I can concentrate and focus on my prayer once I come back." According to the tradition, the time and effort spent by this person on these regular actions then can transform into worship and something pleasing to Allah ﷻ with his or her intention.

Discussion Question

▶   Why is intention more important than the action in practice?

2.   Fears and Stress

One day, the Sufi was thinking about an interesting dream that was a little bit scary. There were rich representations inside her dream. She thought about how she should interpret it. She said to herself, "There is no other way to interpret it but in a good way."

IN PRACTICE

It is important to find people who would positively interpret one's dreams. In one of the sayings of Rasulullah ﷺ Muhammad [28], Allah ﷻ says "I will treat My servant in the way he or she expects Me to be." Therefore, it is always important to have a good opinion of Allah ﷻ. Similarly, if there is a bad dream it is important not to say and publicize it and ask protection from Allah ﷻ from the evils in the dream. Allah ﷻ can do anything. Even if there is a bad destiny written for the person due to the signs in a dream, Allah ﷻ can change an expected bad outcome into a positive one with the divine power.

Discussion Questions

- ► What is the significance of dreams in practice?
- ► What are the guidelines of dream interpretation?

3.   Yesterday and Today

One day, the Sufi was thinking about what she did the previous day. Then thought about what she had done today thus far. She said to herself, "*Alhamdulillah*, thanks to Allah ﷻ, I learned something new today to increase my closeness to Allah ﷻ."

IN PRACTICE

It is very important not to live stagnantly, having a similar or same day without positive change in one's relationship with Allah ﷻ. Rasulullah ﷺ says[29] "The person is not from us, if he or she has the same day consecutively." In other words, every day is an opportunity to increase one's knowledge, practice, and closeness to Allah ﷻ. Other people do not need to know about it and may think that this person is having the same simple life every day. However, one should be able to assess his or her positive self-progress every day in one's relationship with the divine.

Discussion Questions

- ▶ How do people evaluate the progress in their daily encounters?
- ▶ How can one evaluate one's positive or negative change with aging?

4.   Cutting the Grass

There was a Sufi who used to cut the grass in her backyard. As she was cutting the grass with the noisy lawnmower, she used to see bugs jumping frantically around. She used to feel so bad for the bugs she decided to not cut the grass again.

IN PRACTICE

It is very important to respect all of creation. The size of it does not matter. The life is given by Allah ﷻ. One of the attributes of Allah ﷻ is Alive[1] and gives life. This is one of the attributes of Allah ﷻ that Allah ﷻ only manifests but the creation cannot manifest it truly. In other words, Allah ﷻ gives life and people observe things that are moving. If Allah ﷻ made something alive and observable by the person, then he or she is expected to respect this moving creation's freedom of life unless it harms the person.

Discussion Question

> ► How can one make a balance between respecting creation and fulfilling the needs of life?

---

1. *Al-Hayy.*

5.   The Wound

One day, the Sufi was in the restroom. He saw a wound on his body. He did not understand how and from whence it came. He left the restroom, thinking back, when he found the reason for the wound. He immediately prayed, cried, and asked forgiveness from Allah ﷻ. Then, the Sufi sought medical help.

In practice

Whatever happens has a reason. Nothing is random without any cause. There are external and internal meanings for everything. Some people may call this as destiny.[2] In the above story, before seeking medical help, the Sufi immediately looked at an internal possible reason for the wound that appeared on his body. After his contemplation, he correlated the reason for the wound with something that he did that was possibly harmful for his relationship with Allah ﷻ. Therefore, he prayed and asked forgiveness from Allah ﷻ, Real Cause [30]. After this initial step, the Sufi went to the hospital to ask for medical assistance.

Discussion Question

- ► How can one always look for internal and external reasons in different encounters of life?

---

2. Qaza and qadar.

6.   Cancer and the Unknown

One day, the Sufi was thinking of cancer. He said to himself, "Why do people say that there is no cure for cancer? Why do people not know the reason? Why?" As he was thinking all the negative connotations about cancer, he then smiled and said "I understand. The realities, the unknowns, and Allah ﷻ."

In practice

One of the attributes of Allah ﷻ is the Real Cause. Allah ﷻ makes the means such as diseases or cancer to remind a person of their limits and the need for being dependent upon Allah ﷻ. Humans often appear to be more self-confident and independent with the advance of scientific medical research and solutions to diseases. The emergence of cancer-type diseases can be a new way of reminding and challenging the people about their need for Allah ﷻ.

Discussion Question

- What is the understanding of Allah ﷻ in practice in the encounters of evil-seeming incidents?

7. The Cell Phone App and the Happy Old Man

One day, there was an old man sitting in the mosque. The Sufi observed this man. The old man pulled out his cell phone and used the digital counter on his cell phone app to chant. He seemed to be quite happy with his app. He looked around himself to show how much he was proud of the type of advanced technology that he was using, the digital counter! The old man did not realize that a digital counter on a cell phone is an old application but he just found out about it. The Sufi smiled and said to himself, "This is exactly the same in the spiritual path. Everyone thinks that they have the highest level."

IN PRACTICE

At a certain spiritual state, one can think that he or she is at the highest state. But others above him or her can look at this person and can smile like the Sufi in the above story. Therefore, one should always know the possibilities of being in a lower spiritual state than others.

Discussion Question

- How should one ideally view oneself compared to others in practice?

8.   The Harsh Voice

There was a Sufi in Nisantas, Istanbul, Turkey. When he used to talk to his children, they felt that their father was harsh with them. After realizing this after many years, he started communicating with his children by writing on paper and with sign language. His children thought that their father was "cool" and they started talking about him to their friends. The father was happy because now his children loved him and they listened to their dad.

IN PRACTICE

It is very important to tune one's voice in communication. It is very important to be in a soft and calm tone with the people of regular interaction like family members and friends. It is very important to maintain a serious tone in interactions of public life, especially in business. The teaching of tuning down one's voice in communication is often mentioned in the verses of the Qurān, in the practices of the Prophet, and the lives of the saints of Allah ﷻ.[31] One can see the habit of tuning down one's voice as an imitative way of reaching to the genuine way of practicing calmness, softness, mercy, and caring for the entire creation of Allah ﷻ.

Discussion Question

- ▶ What is the long-term expectation of practicing tuning down one's voice?

9.   Oppression and Friends

One day, the Sufi visited her friends late at night. She was very excited to see them. They chanted nicely, ate Sufi treats, and had a great time. The Sufi started talking about her achievements since she did not see her friends for some time. After a while, the Sufi left and went home. She was not able to sleep. Next day, something was bothering her deeply, and she tried to figure out what it was. Finally, she said to herself, "My oppression."

IN PRACTICE

All the good achievements are given by Allah ﷻ to a person. All the evil comes due to the call of the person and thus evil is created. This is a very fine notion to understand, theodicy, the concept of evil in practice. Therefore, the person should be in enormous gratitude to Allah ﷻ by saying, "*Alhamdulillah*, thank you Allah ﷻ" due to being chosen as a simple means for any type of good. If the person claims any ownership of this achievement, then the person in reality lies and oppresses him or herself. Every lie spoils and dirties the sweet relationship with Allah ﷻ. This can make the person disturbed, uneasy and can take the person to a spiritual darkness and misguidance. Therefore, the pronouns "I" or "my" are dangerous pronouns which can take the person to oppression, lying, and arrogance. The statements of "my work," "I achieved," or similar ones are clearly minefields that can backfire upon the person spiritually due to bragging.

Discussion Question

- How can one be selective in using pronouns in daily conversations?

10. Late Night and Evil

There was a Sufi who used to sleep late at night. After having a nice time during most of his time in the day and night, his sleep was much disturbed about the engagements that he did right before he slept. He thought about the reason and solution for this. Then he said to himself, "My dealings late at night!"

In practice

It is important not to involve conversations or any engagements after the last prayer.[3] During these times, there are possibilities of engaging in evil stipulations due to human hormonal changes and existence of other unseen beings released on earth as Rasulullah ﷺ Muhammad mentions in his sayings. There are narrations that mention that Rasulullah ﷺ did not sleep before praying the last prayer and he did not engage in conversations after praying the last prayer[28][20].

Discussion Question

> ► Did you experience a similar case of a bad outcome in a night engagement? How?

---

3. Isha prayer.

11. Candies, the Dirty Guy, and the Sufi

There was a dirty guy who used to come to the mosque. He smelled bad and no one wanted to stay next to him while praying. One day, he came to the Sufi and said, "Here is a bag of candies for your kids." The Sufi did not want to offend him and took the candies from him with thanks. The Sufi thought to himself, "It is probably very old and smelly candies; I won't even open the bag." The Sufi took the bag to his car and kept it there for a few days, afraid to open the bag. One day, he wanted to reward his kids. While he was thinking what to give to them, the Sufi remembered the candies and said, "Let me open the bag to see what it is inside." The Sufi opened the bag and surprisingly, he saw the most expensive brand of candies and chocolates inside. The Sufi reprimanded himself, "My bad thoughts about others. Shame on me!"

IN PRACTICE

It is very important not to judge people according to how they look. There are a lot of sayings in practice that the shabby looking people can be very high in their spiritual levels with Allah ﷻ.[20] It is also very important to have good thoughts about others.

Discussion Question

- ▶ How can one avoid coming to a false conclusion about others?

12. The Fly Catcher

Once there was a big mosque with big glass windows without any openings. Flies used to enter the mosque through the door but got trapped inside, flying against the windowpanes trying to escape. Just before sunset, the Sufi would collect the flies with a paper towel without hurting them and put them outside. She used to take a great pleasure and satisfaction as she saw each of them flying outside freely. She used to say for each freed fly, thirty-three times, "*Alhumdulillah*, thank you Allah ﷻ" to appreciate doing a good deed that Allah ﷻ gave her the ability to do.

IN PRACTICE

All of living creation is precious and respected due to the Creator who gives life. Therefore, it is very important to save a life, as the Sufi above was so happy to save the lives of flies. It is important to recognize that the ability of doing a good deed is from Allah ﷻ. Perhaps the Sufi preferred to do this good deed before sunset because this time is very critical in the practice in increasing one's good deeds. Every day angels present Allah ﷻ the person's daytime deeds before sunset and night deeds after sunrise.[28] Therefore, the Sufi preferred this time for saving the lives of the flies.

Discussion Questions

▶ What is the significance of change in practice?
▶ What does sunset and sunrise signify in one's relationship with Allah ﷻ?

13. Two Prayers

It was the time of the annual festival prayer.[4] People were in dispute about the date of the annual prayer due to disagreements about the lunar calendar. Everyone asked each other in which mosque they followed to pray. If the answer was the questioner's mosque, then they felt happy, but if it wasn't they wanted to argue why their mosque and their date was the right one. The Sufi was watching all these and smiling to herself and saying "*Alhamdulillah*, thanks to Allah ﷻ that there is a difference about the date of the annual prayers, so that I can go both days to a different mosque to pray the annual prayer instead of praying only in one mosque. I wish everyday there was an annual festival prayer in every mosque."

IN PRACTICE

The legal ruling for the annual prayer is praying one time in one mosque once a year. However, in practice, praying to Allah ﷻ is not a burden but a sweet desired engagement with Allah ﷻ. If the person finds different opportunities similar to the Sufi in the above story, he or she can increase those means to derive sweetness in one's relationship with Allah ﷻ.

Discussion Question

► Do the people establish a relationship with Allah ﷻ due to spiritual pleasures or for other reasons?

---

4. Eid prayer.

14.   The Meat-Eater and the Vegetarian

There was a pious Sufi who used to be a farmer in his country and enjoyed eating meat a lot. Then he migrated to America and became an intellectual writer, spending most of his time at a desk in his chair. He still liked eating meat but found himself getting sick often in his new home country with his new occupation. His other Sufi friend was vegetarian and was worried about his friend's health. He always thought that his friend used to get sick because of eating excessive meat. One day, the Sufi who liked meat a lot experienced severe diarrhea and rashes on his skin. His friend advised him, "You really need to change your eating habits. You are not anymore the active farmer Sufi but the one sitting on the chair all the time, so know who you are and adjust your diet accordingly!"

IN PRACTICE

It is important to know who you are and watch what you need and eat. As one's lifestyle changes, a person needs to adapt their eating habits accordingly. Especially in Sufi encounters, a person may need to eat better, worship, and to excel spiritually. If this is not serving the purpose, then this can be a problem.

Discussion Question

▶   What is the importance of food in one's practice?

15.   French Fries and Soda

There was a Sufi who use to attend some Sufi gatherings. At one of these gatherings, some Sufis would eat burgers and French fries with excessive mustard and ketchup washed down with high-fructose sodas. As the Sufi was looking at them, he smiled and wondered to himself, "How can one eat artificial and unhealthy food and still be a Sufi?" Sometime later, one day the Sufi was very hungry, but didn't have any food in his home. A friend happened to stop by and brought some French fries with soda and unhealthy cookies. The Sufi said to himself, "I am so hungry, I will eat." He ate. He felt guilty of breaking his healthy food eating habits but at least he now had some sympathy for the other Sufis at the gathering eating junk food.

IN PRACTICE

It is recommended to eat healthy in order to maintain a healthy bodily and spiritual relationship with Allah ﷻ. It is sometimes acceptable to break the rules to conform with a group if one does not make a big deal of it. This is especially true if a person is invited as a guest—then one is expected to eat whatever is served without acting weird or overly pious.[19]

Discussion Question

▶   What are the etiquettes of being a guest and host?

16. The Angry and Sad Men

It was the day of the year for Muslims for an annual religious festival.[5] The Sufi attended the mosque for prayers. Everyone seemed to be very happy, smiling and greeting each other. Although the Sufi always preferred loneliness and not to socialize, she attended the festival nonetheless. She greeted everyone the same as others. As she was walking out of the building she saw a mother and daughter walking, but they seemed very upset. She saw some angry and sad men as well. The Sufi wanted to greet them but she was scared. She really did not understand and said to herself, "It is really the practice of Rasulullah ﷺ Muhammad not to make others uncomfortable but smile." However, she did not have a good feeling from these people and went home without greeting them. Later she returned to the mosque and though the festival was over, there were still many people there for a funeral. The same people who had looked upset and sad were there: the deceased was their father. The Sufi now understood the reason for their looking unhappy during the festival and felt sad, blaming herself for her quick judgment about others.

In practice

There could be exceptions to all general rules and teachings. Having a funeral on a festival day of joy and happiness can be an exception for some people not to be happy and joyful. Having a genuine empathy for their pain is a virtue and Allah ﷻ rewards the people who have sympathy for the ones with broken hearts due to hardships.

Discussion Question

- ▸ Is it expected to decrease or increase the number of prayers or the amount of worship at the times of holiday, feasts, and festivals? Why?

---

5. Eid.

17. The Young Disciples

There was a Sufi who used to be quite annoyed with her own children. She thought to herself, "How should I change my perspective about them so that I don't get annoyed with my own kids?" Then, she said to herself, "If I see them as students to be trained on the path, then I will expect everything to be normal."

IN PRACTICE

It is important to raise one's children on a spiritual path. Most of the Sufi teachers raise and train their own children as their own disciples.[32] It is a negligence and mistake if one becomes a teacher for others but not for their immediate kinship groups. The best way of teaching is being a role model and increasing the presence with the disciples. The children become like disciples.

Discussion Questions

- ▶ What are the traditional methods of raising one's own children in practice?
- ▶ How can a person balance the roles of being parents and spiritual masters for one's own children?

18.   Spiritual States and Baklava

There was a Sufi who used to love baklava, a sweet treat. As she was excelling in her spiritual states, self-discipline, awareness, and mindfulness journey, she appreciated that while she was eating baklava it tasted very good. Later, she was suffering psychologically upon realizing that baklava was mostly unhealthy. It is high in calories with sugary carbohydrates. The Sufi said to herself, "I need to find treats that are healthy and tasty."

IN PRACTICE

It is really important to be aware and mindful of what one eats.[33] It is not only eating a blessed food but eating healthy and pure food that is important. Keeping the body healthy can make the person more sustainable in one's relationship with Allah ﷻ in quality and quantity measures. Therefore, although one may desire to die and meet with Allah ﷻ, it is also important to have the intention and goal of having a long, healthy life in this world in order to prolong the sweetness of worship and relationship with Allah ﷻ.

Discussion Question

  ▶   What is the relationship between food and worship?

19. The Sufi Teacher and Baklava

Once there was a Sufi teacher. When she was served baklava, she would take one of the delicious pastries, then put it back on the plate without eating it, only licking her fingers. Her disciples watched her to learn practical self-discipline techniques to train the self or ego.

IN PRACTICE

It is important to observe and learn from the teachers. Most of the learning happens when the students or disciples spend time with the teachers in their normal affairs.[34] The genuine teacher lives what she or he teaches. In the above story, the teacher was self-disciplining herself by pretending as if she ate the high-calorie and not fully healthy traditional treat, baklava. She did not totally shun the sweet even though she knew that her ego wanted it. Instead, she let her ego taste it by licking her fingers. Recognizing one's desires and needs of the self or ego is the key and training it accordingly in steps using wisdom makes the person achieve their self-training and spiritual goals.

Discussion Question

▸ What are the other methods of disciplining one's ego?

20. The Radiologist

There was a radiologist who often brought his work home with him. His wife was a Sufi, and due to her husband's work, she used to see at home some of her husband's patients' different internal organs: liver, kidneys, gallbladder, and so forth. She got surprised, sometimes disgusted, and sometimes had feelings of awe. One day, she thought to herself, "Why are people physically attracted to each other? Their internal organs are all the same . . ."

IN PRACTICE

It is important to recognize that externalities do not mean anything. Although Allah ﷻ created all humans perfect and beautiful in their external appearances, what matters in the spiritual journey is the internal piety of love, respect, and appreciation of Allah ﷻ. This notion is called *taqwa*. This concept is much emphasized in both the Qurān and the sayings of the Prophet. Rasulullah ﷺ says "Allah ﷻ does not value your physical appearances but values what is in your hearts and actions. [20]" The verse of the Qurān mentions that Allah ﷻ created different ethnicities and genders to know each other and to maximize *taqwa* with diverse interactions.[viii]

Discussion Question

> ► What is the relationship between the internal and external in practice?

21. Dark Monday

The Sufi woke up Monday morning. It was dark. When she looked outside from the window, she immediately felt pain and longing for travel to another place. But she could not do it because she needed to go to work the next day. She said to herself, "Fasting! I know it will be a little bit painful but the result will be good for sure."

In practice

One of the ways to change one's perspective in life is through fasting. Fasting is from sunrise to sunset without intake of any food or drink. Fasting, as recommended by Rasulullah ﷺ on Mondays and Thursdays, helps the person to discipline her or his ego and self. Accordingly, the person can have a better perspective in mind, body, and life. If the person performs fasting only for Allah ﷻ as a ritual, Allah ﷻ rewards the person in this world and the afterlife according to the Prophetic narration.[28][20] All the genuine struggles to train one's raw ego is awarded by Allah ﷻ if it is done correctly.

Discussion Question

 ▸   How does fasting help change one's perspective?

22.   Store Closing, the Sufi, and the Deal

One day, while the Sufi was driving her car, she saw a store that was closing. She went into the store and bought a few items. An item usually worth $100 was sold for $1. She bought a few items and thought that she got a great deal. She planned to share the deal she got with her friends and family. Then for a minute she stopped and started thinking about the owner of the store. She felt sad about the owner and how possibly the owner was going through bankruptcy. She said to herself, "I wish I bought it for its normal price and did not feel so bad for the owner. It is so sad. I now understand the Real Owner gives much without losing."

IN PRACTICE

It is very important to have sympathy for others for their losses. If someone is losing and others are benefiting from that loss and gaining, then it is not a real gain. The sincerity of a person should dictate asking, praying, and desiring good for everyone. Allah ﷻ as the Real Owner can give very expensive and precious goods in this life and in the afterlife for a very cheap price if the person makes a simple effort to buy it.

Discussion Question

▶   What is the concept of spiritual bankruptcy?

23.   On the Floor of the Mosque

One day the Sufi lied on the floor on the carpet in the mosque. He was tired, and felt as though he fell asleep, but was at the same time awake. He was aware of noises around him, but when he tried to get up, he was unable to. He gave orders to his body, but his body was not listening to him. He thought, "Now I understand what death is like. The body dies but not the soul."

IN PRACTICE

It is important to understand what death is. When a person dies, his or her physical body dies but this person's soul does not die. The frame of the body is not under the command chain of the soul anymore. There are narrations from Rasulullah ﷺ that buried dead people can hear the people around them from the grave.[20] In the Qurãn, it is mentioned that sleeping is similar to death as well.[viiiii] In the above story, the Sufi was in the state of half sleep and half awake. There is a special name for this state.[6] The Sufi in this state rationalized the relationship between the soul and body through his own experience.

Discussion Question

 ▸   What is the relationship between sleep and death?

---

6. *Yaqaza* means the mixed state of sleep and awareness.

24. Difficult People

There was a Sufi who used to lose his temper when dealing with difficult people. After each time he lost his temper, he regretted it and said to himself, "I wish I was patient; I wish I didn't say that, I wish I didn't talk too much . . . I wish. I wish . . ."

IN PRACTICE

It is important to control oneself through trial and error, repentance, and asking forgiveness from Allah ﷻ. Rasulullah ﷺ once asked who was the most powerful person in a patriarchal society. Everyone present in the gathering answered that it was the muscular person who could knock down his enemies in a fight. Rasulullah ﷺ replied, "No, it is the person who can control his or her anger."[28]

Discussion Question

- ► How can one compare anger management techniques with the teachings of Islam?

25. Enemy Advice

There was a woman who wrote her first book. Everyone gave her advice on how to make the book better. Her Sufi friend gave her advice also on how to improve the book. The author thought that everyone was jealous of her, therefore they were criticizing her book. The Sufi said to her, "Look! If everyone is saying the same thing about your book, then you should really stop seeing them as your enemy and appreciate what they say and improve it."

In practice

It is important not to see people as enemies, haters, or jealousy banks when they give advice. Creating imaginary adversaries only increases one's own arrogance due to not accepting any criticism. It is important to improve oneself even though others may not have a sincere intention when giving advice. Jealousy is always possible and real in practice. There are litanies and prayers to be protected from the evil eye.

Discussion Question

- ► Why it is difficult to accept criticism from others about oneself?

26. Crooked Advice

One day, the Sufi asked advice of his friend about helping a person in need. His friend suggested some ways of helping but they did not seem ethical and honest. The Sufi felt uneasy at the idea of the crooked suggestions. His friend kept insisting that there is nothing wrong if the end result is good, and that it is OK to cheat. The Sufi kept saying that was not right. The communication went back and forth without any result.

IN PRACTICE

It is important to reach a virtuous act through virtuous and ethical steps. A person gains power and strength from being honest and just in all his or her affairs. Doing everything ethically with consciousness of Allah ﷻ can reward the person in this world and in the afterlife. There are a lot of cases that a true, honest person may not be appreciated by one's peers, friends, or family members but only truly appreciated by Allah ﷻ.

Discussion Question

- ► How do you explain the above statement "reaching a virtuous act through virtuous and ethical steps"?

27.   The Kids and Candies

There was a Sufi whose wife bought boxes of candy snacks for their children to take to school. The snacks were healthy organic ones, but expensive. His wife used to put the candies in the fridge and pantry, accessible to the kids. Quite often the Sufi would hear his wife chiding the kids for finishing the snacks at home leaving nothing for the next day's lunch bags. The Sufi listened to her, smiled and said to himself, "If the candies are accessible then it is normal to finish."

IN PRACTICE

Spiritual candies are given by Allah ﷻ as an encouragement for the traveler on the journey.[35] If a person has the choice of getting the candies, then the candies will not survive and finish. Therefore, one should know that all the spiritual candies[7] or miracles are given and controlled by Allah ﷻ. The person does not have any control over them unless the person is enabled or empowered by Allah ﷻ. This is even true for the prophets. The prophets can show miracles or spiritual candies as long as Allah ﷻ empowers them and gives them the ability to do so. Therefore no one can claim ability of divinity except Allah ﷻ. In one of the chapters of the Qurān, Rasulullah ﷺ mentions his humanness, and that if he knew what would be in the future, then he would increase his good deeds. No one knows the future except Allah ﷻ.

Discussion Question

> ▸ How do you interpret the concept of "spiritual candies" in your personal life encounters?

---

7. *Karamahs* in Arabic are spiritual candies as a terminology in Sufism.

28. Going to the Bathroom before Sleep

There was a Sufi who used to go to the bathroom before going to sleep. He felt that if he didn't, then his body's organs would complain and ruin all of the homeostasis he worked for. Some nights he did not want to go to the bathroom but he did anyway out of habit. One night, he was so tired he slept without going to the bathroom first. The next day when he woke up he did not feel well. He said to himself, "Now, I will hear all day the internal complaints."

In practice

The body parts can complain in this life and the afterlife. In the Qurãn,[viii][iv] it is mentioned that some of the body parts of a person will talk and witness against the person. In the above story, the Sufi considered each of his body parts as a separate individual and tried to fulfill their needs.

Discussion Question

- ► How can one identify oneself if his or her organs take a position against this person? In other words, how do you define "self"?

29.   The Low Voice

There was a Sufi who used to think that most of her problems with her family and friends were due to her loud, intimating voice. Therefore, before talking she used to make an effort to lower and dim the tone of her voice. As soon as she did that, she realized people were much nicer, warmer, and more gentle to her. One day, she forgot to do it while she was in conversation with her friend. She looked at her friend's face and saw that she got really irritated and annoyed. Immediately, she changed her voice to the low and dim tone. Her friend started smiling and shaking her head in agreement about their discussion.

IN PRACTICE

It is important to control one's voice tone while speaking with others, especially if it is other fellow spiritual travelers, teachers, or parents. There is a teaching in the Qurān[ixvvi] about this manner and etiquette when talking to Rasulullah ﷺ in a lower and softer voice.

Discussion Questions

- ► How do you interpret the concept of voice tone, low or high pitch?
- ► How is one's voice tone related to one's spiritual disposition?

30. Self-Struggle, the Goal, and the Sufi

One morning as the Sufi woke up, she was thinking: "What should I eat or drink so that it does not bother me later in the day so that I can still nicely worship Allah ﷻ today? How should I not lose my temper with my kids as they are preparing for the school yelling and screaming so that I can still nicely worship Allah ﷻ today? How should I text and e-mail my colleague about work so that it does not bother me later and I can still nicely worship Allah ﷻ today?"

IN PRACTICE

This is the goal: self–struggle.[8] The goal is not struggling and fighting with others but struggling and controlling oneself for betterment in the journey to Allah ﷻ. In the Qurān, it mentions for Rasulullah ﷺ Abraham that he meets Allah ﷻ in the state of calm heart, free from the spiritual diseases.[9] Rasulullah ﷺ reminds his companions that when they come from a self–defense physical fight that this was a minor struggle compared to the one when a person struggles with him or herself.[28][20]

Discussion Questions

- ► How do you interpret the concept of self-struggle?
- ► Do you think that it is more difficult to deal with oneself compared to others? Why?

---

8. *Jihad.*
9. Qalbun Saliim.

31.   The Worried Sufi

There was a Sufi who used to be worried about the unknowns of the day when she used to wake up. She used to be very uncomfortable and wondering what to do. Then she said to herself, "I will do everything as best as I can ethically and pleasing to Allah ﷻ and then I will show reliance in Allah ﷻ. I won't lie. I will be honest. I won't oppress anyone or myself. I won't break anyone's heart. I won't waste my time and will use as much as I can for worshipping Allah ﷻ." After making those promises, she felt good and said to herself "*Alhamdulillah*, at least I made the intention *inshAllah*."

IN PRACTICE

Every day is a new opportunity with unknowns, possibly with evil and good-looking incidents. There are daily prayers of Rasulullah ﷺ Muhammad to be performed before sunrise and sunset because each new day starts with sunset in the lunar calendar. These prayers are performed especially thanking Allah ﷻ after immediately before or after sunset and sunrise, asking protection from all the evils and asking blessings for that day. Intention is the key in all the actions. If someone makes the intention, as the Sufi in the above story, then intention itself is the biggest prayer to Allah ﷻ. Lastly, when everyone does in his or her capacity the struggles as the promises of the Sufi in the above story, then the people should not take much more burden on themselves but truly and fully rely on Allah ﷻ. This concept is known as *tawakkul* in practice which means doing as best as you can then, having reliance on Allah ﷻ.[36]

Discussion Questions

- ▶ How can one apply the concept of "tawakkul" in daily regular engagements?
- ▶ Do you consider that starting the day with a prayer is important? Why?

32. The Intellectuals

One day a Sufi attended an intellectual religious gathering where people discussed various issues. The Sufi said, "The religious sciences cannot be discussed as normal social sciences. One should have a holistic approach of respect, and humility in attitude and in language even when one is expressing different opinions on an issue." The people seemed to be offended with the Sufi's logic. They said, "We are intellectuals. We can discuss in a modern and in an unlimited way so that religious sciences can flourish like other sciences. That is the reason why religion is backwards! It does not apply the modern ways!" The Sufi smiled and left the gathering.

In practice

It is important to distinguish the religious sciences from others. Especially if the Divine knowledge is the topic of discussion, then one should adapt the proper etiquettes of words, thoughts, and movements. This helps a person learn, apply, and improve. Sufis' silent moments are filled with deep satisfactory and respectable reflection of Allah ﷻ. Their words are the statements of pearls deeply penetrating to the hearts. It is not being a good speaker that is important, but having the proper etiquette with Allah ﷻ.

Discussion Questions

- How do you define the concept of "intellectuals" in the story?
- Do the spiritual followers use the term "intellectuals" for their experts in the field? Why?

33. The Cool Car

The Sufi mom had a cheap car. Her kids always thought that their mother had the coolest car. They said to her, "Mom! You have such a nice car. My friends think that either you have a Ferrari, Porsche, or Tesla. But it's even cooler than those!" The Sufi smiled to herself, "If they knew the value of this car compared to the ones that they are talking about, they would be disappointed!"

In practice

In one's relationship with Allah ﷻ, people may have very high opinion about a person. They may see this person as a saint or friend of Allah ﷻ. In essence, the person knows himself or herself. Putting false clothes on oneself without realizing it can lead to lies and arrogance. Therefore, there is the prayer of Rasulullah ﷺ "Oh Allah ﷻ! Please elevate my status in the eyes of people and lower my status in my own eyes.[37]" Rasulullah ﷺ asks elevated status in people's eyes because he wants people to respect and listen to his message from Allah ﷻ. However, he teaches us to look upon our own selves with lower value not to be arrogant. Rasulullah ﷺ asked Allah ﷻ to embody this understanding in himself and taught others to follow the same path.

Discussion Question

▶ Why do we have a tendency to be proud of our children or our group identities?

34. Texting and Driving

There was a Sufi who was driving. He saw a driver in the next lane who was texting on her phone while driving. After a few seconds, the woman did not see the car stopping in front of her. She almost hit the car in front of her but finally stopped just before doing so. The Sufi looked at her face. She looked fearful, stressed, and pale after being saved from an accident. The Sufi smiled and said to himself, "I don't understand these people. In this stressful life, these people put more unnecessary stress on themselves by texting and driving. Instead of enjoying the road, the trees, and different scenes while driving and being with Allah ﷻ, they want to put more stress on themselves. I don't understand!"

IN PRACTICE

It is important to use every opportunity to benefit in one's relationship with Allah ﷻ. Focused driving while enjoying the nature, silence, and making chants are some of the ways some Sufis discharge themselves from the fears, stress, and anxieties of the day. In the above story, the Sufi witnessed an opposite case by another driver. She put stress upon herself by texting on her phone while driving. The Sufi did not find this texting practice logical.

Discussion Questions

- ▶ How can one make driving enjoyable?
- ▶ Why are some of the activities considered distracting in driving compared to others?
- ▶ How do you interpret the concept of self-reflection, silence, and chanting while driving?

35.   The Stingy Sufi and the Ice Cream

There was a stingy Sufi who took her kids and her friend out for ice cream. Her friend was delayed for the ice cream party. She said to herself, "Let me buy the ice cream before my friend comes. If she comes later she can pay for her own ice cream." She bought the ice cream for her kids and started eating with them. After a few minutes, her friend arrived. The Sufi was embarrassed and said to her friend, "Let me buy your ice cream too as I promised." Her friend ordered her ice cream. The Sufi was about to pay for the ice cream when the owner of the store said, "She is on me. You don't need to pay for her." The Sufi thanked the owner and felt embarrassed about her thoughts.

IN PRACTICE

It is important to be generous. Allah ﷻ gives much to people and does not ask anything in return except the recognition and appreciation of the One and only Allah ﷻ. In the above story, the Sufi had a spiritual sickness of being stingy and fear of spending on others. Allah ﷻ sent her a sign, then she felt bad and embarrassed about this issue.

Discussion Question

- ▶ Why is generosity considered as virtuous compared to being stingy?

36. Teachers and Gratefulness

One day, the Sufi was upset and disturbed about the ungratefulness of people about their teachers. She had a friend who was complaining about her teacher who did a lot for her. She said to herself, "I don't understand. You benefited a lot from your teacher. Now, you see something you don't like and you don't agree as if your teacher did not do anything for you." The Sufi was very sad about the ungratefulness of people for their teachers.

In practice

The people that we benefit from have rights on us. The first gratefulness is expected for Allah ﷻ, then for parents, then for teachers. It is not ethical or fair to act ungrateful, as when the person does not recognize and appreciate the benefits that one receives from one's teacher.

Discussion Question

  ▶ Why is being ungrateful not a noble trait?

37. The Bald Head and the Ponytail

There was a Sufi who used to always shave his head. He preferred to have a bald head because he liked having short hair. The Sufi also did not have time and effort to take care of long hair. He knew that if he had long hair it would be a mess all the time. He never understood how a man could have a ponytail and used to talk badly about them. One day, he looked at the mirror. He realized that he was losing his hair and some part of his head had already become bald. He was sad despite always shaving his hair. He decided to not cut nor shave his hair anymore because soon enough his head would be naturally bald due to the hair loss. After a year, his hair grew long and now he had a ponytail. He looked at the mirror. He did not like the look of himself with the ponytail, but he did not want to cut it because soon he would lose all his hair. Now, the Sufi was preserving his ponytail although he did not like it.

IN PRACTICE

It is important to appreciate all the favors from Allah ﷻ before we lose them. The first favor is existence with good health. Another favor is knowing Allah ﷻ and having the ability to pray to Allah ﷻ. Another favor is having strength to walk, to eat, to breath, to sleep, to think, and so forth. When we get sick or when we lose some of those abilities we tend to look at people with the abilities and to be envious of them. Another important point in the above story is the situations, responsibilities, or people that we don't like much. Once we come to know that we can lose them we start grasping or holding them tight. Therefore, the spiritual state of appreciation is very important in practice. Allah ﷻ especially gives Rasulullah ﷺ Muhammad a high status due to his constant mode of appreciation for Allah ﷻ. Therefore, the word or title "Muhammad" means the one who always appreciates and thanks Allah ﷻ.

Discussion Question

> ► Why do we tend to attach value to things once we realize that we will soon lose them?

38.   The Headache

One day, the Sufi woke up with a severe headache. She was in much pain and wondered about the possible reasons for the headache. She avoided taking any medicine until she performed some spiritual healing and talismanic practice. She went to the bathroom to make ablutions,[10] washed up herself with sacred teachings. Then she started praying. She felt a little better but the headache was still there. She started reading some talismanic verses from the last three chapters of the Qurãn. After reading thrice, she blew on her hands and wiped her body with her hands as Rasulullah ﷺ suggested.[38] She felt even better but still she had some traces of the headache. As she wondered what type of painkilling pills she should take, or if she would just bear the pain, she decided upon doing some Prophetic suggested prayers for illness. Then, she fell asleep and after a while woke up feeling much better. She said, "*Alhamdulillah,* thanks to Allah ﷻ, I didn't need the medicine."

IN PRACTICE

It is important to consult Allah ﷻ in any issue or problem before seeking assistance from other means. Other means can help as long as Allah ﷻ empowers them. In the above story, painkiller pills can be considered as "other means" for headache. One can take it but should remember that the cure is still given by Allah ﷻ. The Sufi did not need to consult to other means and she only used the talismanic readings from the Qurãn[39] and litanies of Rasulullah ﷺ to ask help from Allah ﷻ. If they did not work out she could have taken the medicine and ask Allah ﷻ to make the pills sufficient or remedy for her headache.

Discussion Question

- ▸ What should be the disposition of a person when he or she first expresses their need to Allah ﷻ?

---

10. *Wudhu.*

39. The Mosque's Wooden Table

There was a small wooden table in the mosque. People in the mosque used to put the garbage can on this table. One day, the Sufi was looking for a table to put the Qurãn on and to read from it. There were no tables in the mosque except the plastic ones. As the Sufi always preferred natural pieces, she did not want to put the Qurãn on a plastic table. As she searched, she saw the wooden table with a garbage can on top of it. The Sufi smiled and said to herself, "Now, your status will be elevated and noble, *inshAllah*, with the will of Allah ﷻ." She cleared, cleaned, and perfumed the table. Then she put the Qurãn on it to read it. After a few months, this wooden table became the most wanted and preferred table in the mosque for reading the Qurãn. No one wanted to use the plastic ones. One day, the Sufi entered the mosque, two people were fighting for this table. The Sufi looked at the scene and said, "Garbage history, nobility and fame, and the elevation of Allah ﷻ."

In practice

Sometimes we don't realize or take into consideration a person's past when we criticize them. On the spiritual path especially, everyone has a garbage history. Even the selected people of Allah ﷻ, the messengers or prophets, were guided to a better spiritual state after receiving revelation from Allah ﷻ. When a person is elevated by Allah ﷻ to a noble level the person should always be humble, thankful, and appreciative of Allah ﷻ's favors and remember his or her past. It is known in the Muslim history that Arabs were desert and tribal people with unhuman renderings and dealings. It is much of the appreciation of early Muslims[11] to always remember their past and appreciate Allah ﷻ's guidance to humanity and civility with the advent of Islam. This appreciation made them advance rapidly in the early Islamic period compared to later periods in the history when people received or inherited the religion from their parents as a culture.

Discussion Question

 ► Who or what determines the value of things?

---

11. *Sahabah.*

40. The Long-Haired Brother and the Bald Brother

There was a Sufi who had a bald friend. People used to refer to him as the "brother with bald hair." This man used to get annoyed with this description until finally he got some surgical hair implants. After a few years, his hair grew long and people started calling him the "brother with long hair." He was now happy and confident about his new nickname. The Sufi observed this change in his friend's approach and smiled and said to himself, "What others think; does it matter?"

IN PRACTICE

It is important not to worry about others' opinion especially if it is related to the externalities. Looks or bodily appearances are one of the traps that people fall in without understanding the essence of the existence of a person. Therefore, there may be some Sufis who may not care what others think. There may be other Sufis who can try to fit into the similar outlook of their culture so that they look normal and ordinary like others.

Discussion Question

▶   What are different positions in one's outlook in practice?

41. Seeking Guidance

Over many years, the Sufi was wondering, "Why do some people have guidance and know about Allah ﷻ?" One day, he visited one of her friends who was very rich. He was a new Sufi. The new Sufi was so humble that he even saw children as her teachers. The older Sufi said, "I found the answer: Humility!"

IN PRACTICE

Allah ﷻ can inspire an answer to a question after many years if the person has a genuine struggle and intention of learning. It is not unusual to see Sufi stories about a Sufi master struggling with his or herself about a dilemma and years later, the answer can be given by Allah ﷻ. The concept of guidance in practice appears often with the traits of humbleness and humility. There may be people who can know orthodoxy, the right or authentic path but due to the identity, group ownerships, arrogance or other reasons they may not have orthopraxy, the right practice. Similarly, Satan was very intelligent as mentioned in various the Qurān but he always lost due to his lack of humility.

Discussion Question

- ▶ Why do you think humility is one of the important keys for guidance?

42. The Lazy Sufi

There was a Sufi who used to read her protection prayers and litanies in the morning and night. One day, she was lazy and was not able to wake up in the morning to read and perform her prayers before she left home for work. She had a very bad day. At the end of day, she was realized the reason for having such a bad day. She said to herself, "My laziness about my protection prayers."

IN PRACTICE

It is very important not to start and enter the day and night before one engages, reads, and protects themselves with prayers.[40] If someone misses them, it is normal and expected for an evil to happen in that person's day. It is expected to have reliance on Allah ﷻ regularly through prayers for protection from evil and bad outcomes.[41]

Discussion Question

▶   Why are the protection prayers or litanies very critical?

43. One Hand, One Leg, One Eye

There was a Sufi who used to practice having one hand, one leg, or one eye for part of each month. She would put one of her hands in a cast for a week and use only one of her hands. The next month, she used crutches to walk and to do her work and daily needs with one leg. The following month she put a cover on one of her eyes in order to only use one of her eyes for her daily needs and at work. The Sufi did not tell anyone this secret. She was pretending as if an accident or something happened to her. Except one day, a friend deduced the Sufi's secret practice, and asked for the Sufi's reason. The Sufi said, "I will tell you the reason only because you probably think I am crazy. I want to appreciate what Allah ﷻ gave me. Sometimes, I see people around and they don't appreciate what Allah ﷻ gives them and Allah ﷻ tests them with difficulties. I want to truly feel this appreciation for Allah ﷻ before any trial or evil hits me. You may still think that I am crazy but it doesn't matter."

In practice

It is really important to be in constant appreciation and in constant gratitude for the favors of Allah ﷻ. Most of the time, people value what they lose. People are envious of what they don't have. In the above story, the Sufi was trying to instruct and train her own ego for this true sense of appreciation of Allah ﷻ.

Discussion Question

▶ Why do people tend to look at others and notice what the others have but they don't have?

44.   The Dirty Coffee Machine

One day, the Sufi wanted to make coffee. She started pouring water from another container into the coffee water tank in order to fill it. As she was pouring, the container's cap fell on the ground. The Sufi pondered the message of the falling cap. After she finished pouring the water, she looked into the container and saw dirt in the bottom of the container. Then, she smiled and said to herself, "This is the message." She dumped the water, cleaned the tank, and filled it with a clean container.

IN PRACTICE

There is a meaning and sign in every minute detail of life. Everything happens with an external and internal reason. If a person does not ignore these signs, then he or she can use everything and every moment for their advantage. Then life's incidents become more purposeful with awareness. These positive signs can come from Allah ﷻ as long as the person has the intention and struggle to regularly maintain the prayers to Allah ﷻ.[39]

Discussion Question

> ▸   Can there be a meaning for every simple incident in one's life?

45.   Remembering Role Models

One day, the Sufi was feeling uneasy. She did not act in a way that her teacher wanted her to act. She was remembering the days that she spent with her teacher. Her teacher was a true role model. She was gentle, nice, and patient. She did not rush to correct people's mistakes. She used wisdom in her style of communication. The Sufi considered all of these and she was ashamed of herself for her inadequacies, and said to herself, "It is difficult, but I guess this is the struggle and self-improvement."

IN PRACTICE

It is very important to try to better oneself. Realization of mistakes is the first step to change. One should not give up the struggle because it is difficult. Teachers as role models are present to show to their students that it can be done and there are other humans who can achieve some results at the end of self-struggle. In all stages of life, one should always humbly ask assistance and guidance from Allah ﷻ in different types of self-struggle.

Discussion Questions

- ► What is the place of good teachers?
- ► What are the signs of a good teacher?

46. Weakness and Power

Lately the Sufi was feeling weak and old although she was still in good health and young. She wondered if it was related to the type of food that she had been eating or she was missing taking some of her vitamins. Then she thought about some of the Sufis who were eighty or ninety years old but were still active like young people. They were involved with good groups and social work and spent a good amount of their time worshipping and praying to Allah ﷻ. Then she smiled and said to herself, "Maybe that is the reason: they pray and ask from Allah ﷻ constantly to be active and to have energy for the good deeds and worship."

IN PRACTICE

One of the prayers that is recited after each prayer is asking Allah ﷻ to help the person worship and pray to Allah ﷻ in an easy and enjoyable manner.[42] This prayer is one of the famous prayers of Rasulullah ﷺ Muhammad. As the person faces different challenges in life with age, health, and different life-related conditions, the energy or the zeal for worship and doing good may not be at the desired level all the time. Therefore, it is very important to ask Allah ﷻ to enable the person to be involved with the good actions and worship until one dies.

Discussion Question

- ▸ What is the importance of prayers or asking one's needs constantly from Allah ﷻ?

47. The Disconnected Traveler

One day, a Sufi teacher was teaching about the importance of disconnection. One student was chanting the Divine phrases and praying. He became disconnected from his surrounding and was set to begin spiritual travel. Then after a while he reconnected with his surroundings after the chanting was over. The teacher explained charge and discharge in chanting, and how one should focus on himself rather than the noises, lights, temperature, or anything in the physical environment.

In practice

It is very important to focus while performing the chants. One of the famous chants is *La ilaha illa Allah*. The person tries to take everything out of his or her mind and heart and focus only on the One and Only Creator, Allah. By doing so, the person discharges themselves from all worries, stresses, anxieties, and fears.[22]

Discussion Question

- ▶ Is it possible to disconnect from one's surroundings in a crowded environment where there are a lot of distractions? Why?

48. The Loud Greeter

There was a man who used to greet everyone very loudly in the mosque. When this man approached the Sufi, the Sufi pretended that he was doing his prayers in order not to be disturbed. After a while, everyone in the mosque started greeting each other loudly. The Sufi smiled and said to himself, "Even though I don't like it, I think this man started something good as a practice. At least people are greeting each other and not grumbling."

IN PRACTICE

It is important to greet each other and smile. Rasulullah ﷺ recommends one of the rights of a person over another is greeting each other nicely when they see each other[20]. However, some Sufis, as in the above story, prefer silence and solitude. The Sufi avoided socializing but when he saw that the loud greeter encouraged others to increase the practice of greeting, he critiqued and disagreed with his own self and applauded the achievement of the man for starting something good.

Discussion Questions

- ▶ What is the effect of greeting in social life?
- ▶ What is the effect of greeting in spiritual life?

49. The Professor

There was a Sufi who used to teach at a college. She felt that some of the students were treating her in a disrespectful way. She said to herself, "I need to be patient." As the semester was getting close to the end, the Sufi gained empathy for these students and made good friends with them. After the semester was over, one of the students wrote a reflection about the Sufi's class that it was his best class in the college. When the Sufi read this she said to herself, "After every difficulty there is an ease."

IN PRACTICE

It is important to be patient in all different walks of life. Husband–wife relationships, student–teacher relationships, parent–children relationships, and friend relationships: all require patience to be successful and to have long life effects. In the above story, the Sufi had empathy for her students' not respectful behaviors which helped her actualize and apply patience in her relationship with them. After this self-struggle, as Allah ﷻ mentions in the Qurān[x] after each difficulty there is an ease that rewards the person's self-struggle in the form of patience both in this world with positive results and in the afterlife if the person had a right and good intention.

Discussion Question

- ▸ What is the wisdom of having a difficulty after an ease and having an ease after a difficulty in circular days destined by Allah ﷻ?

50.   Tea for the Traveler

One day, a stranger who was mentally ill visited the mosque. Everyone was fasting but the stranger did not know about it. He made tea and wanted to show his generosity and gave a cup of tea to the Sufi. The Sufi said that he was fasting. The stranger insisted that the Sufi needed to take the tea cup from him. The Sufi did not want to argue and took it from him and put it to the side. The Sufi thought to himself, "What is the message?" After a while, a traveler who was not fasting came to the mosque looking tired. The Sufi said to himself, "Now, I get the message." He gave the tea to the traveler. The traveler was happy and the Sufi smiled.

IN PRACTICE

There is a meaning in everything. Nothing is haphazard if a person can understand it. Travelers, the sick, and mentally ill are all exempt from fasting. In the above story, the Sufi did not want to argue with the stranger who was mentally ill because there was no use. On the other hand, the Sufi did not understand why this happened until the traveler came to the mosque. Then, the Sufi found a meaning in this small incident.

Discussion Questions

- Is it possible to understand the real reason behind every evil or good seeming incident if one is patient?
- How can one define the notion of "the real reason" behind every incident?

51. Breaking the Fast

There was a Sufi who used to have a difficult time with fasting. When she went without any food and drink she often got headaches. Breaking the fast was enjoyable for her, however; it was a spiritual achievement. With this dilemma of pain and joy, she always had a hard time deciding if she should fast or not. She said to herself, "I can do anything but I can't do without coffee." As the sunset time came, she used to forget all the pain that she went through the day due to fasting. She used to say "*Alhamdulillah*, thanks to Allah ﷻ for another achievement." She grew confident, happy, and focused after fasting.

IN PRACTICE

One of the difficult practices that can be a good way of disciplining the self or ego is fasting. The ritual of fasting is having no food, drink, and spousal intimate relationship from sunrise to sunset. In tradition, all the spiritual efforts are rewarded by Allah ﷻ. In the sayings of the Prophet, Allah ﷻ rewards the fasting person in a special manner compared to the other forms of worship in practice. Rasulullah ﷺ says, "The fasting person has two rewards: one at the time of breaking the fast and the other is in the afterlife, amazed with enormous awards from Allah ﷻ.[28] [20]" The Sufi in the above story experienced the utmost pleasure and happiness at the time of breaking the fast as the initial reward mentioned by the Prophet. She felt good, focused, confident, and happy after this spiritual achievement.

Discussion Question

► How does fasting help the person to focus and collect one's spiritual messiness?

52. Children, Patience, and Prayer

There was a Sufi who used to get easily annoyed with his children. He used to yell and scream at them, especially when they used to make a mess in the house. After a while, he used to feel bad and said to himself, "I wish I was patient and could be nicer to my kids." Every day, it was the same scenario: first, yelling and screaming, then feeling bad about his treatment of his kids. One day, he said to himself, "I am making myself miserable with this situation. I need to do something." Then, he said to himself, "Let me pray." He prayed and asked help from Allah ﷻ for his situation. After a while, he smiled and said, "*Alhamdulillah*, I know what to do now. I need to practice my patience but I can't be patient unless I am strong. But I can't be strong unless I make my relationship with Allah ﷻ stronger through more prayers."

IN PRACTICE

Patience is not a virtual concept.[43] This trait solidifies in one's character with constant and regular prayers. Therefore, a minimum of five times prayer exists. Depending on the need and the situation of the person, one can increase these daily engagements to be more spiritually strong. In the above story, the Sufi needed to embody the notion of patience. He realized his shortcomings. He was constantly doing self-struggle and blaming his own ego and self. One of the praiseworthy steps in spiritual journey is the state of the self or ego when it realizes its mistakes and puts blame on it instead of blaming others. The next step comes after the diagnosis of the spiritual disease, and its treatment is reached through knowledge and practice. The Sufi realized that one of the ways in the practice is to embody patience through prayers.

Discussion Questions

- ► How can daily regular prayers embody patience in one's spiritual strength?
- ► What are the levels of self or ego in practice?

53. Hugging at the Airport

There was a Sufi who came from overseas to visit his friend. Many years had passed since they had last seen each other. His friend was waiting outside the airport to pick up the Sufi. As soon as the Sufi came out from the airport, he saw the Sufi. Both the Sufi and his friend were very happy to see each other and they had a few tears in both of their eyes. The overseas Sufi greeted his friend and gave him a hug but the local Sufi was not comfortable and said to his friend, "In this country, if two men hug each other it may have some other meanings." His Sufi friend from overseas asked what he meant, and his friend replied, "I will explain it later."

In practice

When people greet each other, some hug regardless of gender. Same-sex hugging or holding hands walking on the streets does not mean that they have sexual relationships. These are the ways of showing their close friendships as practiced in some of the Sufi cultures. It is also common to cry among men when they see a friend who was absent for a long time. The reason for crying is to express happiness or joy for reunion.

Discussion Question

- How can one interpret the famous relationship between Rumi and his teacher Shams?

54.   The Serious Sufi and the Smiling Sufi

There were two Sufi friends. One was always serious and the other was always funny and making jokes. One day, the serious Sufi asked the funny Sufi, "Why do you always make jokes although what we deal with is very serious? The afterlife, death, accountability, prayer, etc. . . ." The smiling Sufi smiled and said, "My exterior may be funny but inside I am burning serious."

IN PRACTICE

It is important not to make people uncomfortable even though the spiritual journey is very important and serious. Most of the time, the separation between the pious and non-pious can be due to their external interactions. In practice, all the internal interactions which is the essence of the spiritual journey is only undertaken for Allah ﷻ and to please Allah ﷻ. Rasulullah ﷺ used to say: "If you knew what I knew, then you would laugh less but cry a lot.[28][20]" Yet Rasulullah ﷺ used to sit with people and listen to their jokes and smile. Sometimes, he also used to make jokes with the contents of wisdom and truth. Rasulullah ﷺ did not make people feel uncomfortable or cold. The Qurān praises this quality of Rasulullah ﷺ and mentions that if Rasulullah ﷺ was harsh, then the people would not be around him as much, as they loved to be around him.[xivii]

Discussion Questions

- ▶ How can one balance between the real self and external self?
- ▶ Can one consider external self as fake if it does not match with internal self? Why?
- ▶ Why do people often tend not to like serious people?

55. The Sleeping Stranger

There was once a man who had been sleeping at nights in the mosque for a few weeks. This was a man that people in the mosque did not know much about, and they were uncomfortable with this stranger. One day, while there was only the Sufi and the stranger, the Sufi approached him and asked if he was the son of a woman who had passed away two weeks ago. The man said, "yes." The Sufi said to himself, "Now, everything makes sense." The next day, the man was sleeping in the mosque again. One of the administrators of the mosque was a harsh man and reprimanded the stranger, saying, "This is a mosque. You cannot sleep at night here." The Sufi witnessed this and felt bad for the stranger. After the prayer finished in the mosque, the Sufi took a courageous step and made an announcement in the mosque. He introduced the stranger to everyone and explained why he was sleeping in the mosque.

IN PRACTICE

It is very important to have empathy for people. The Sufi with Divine guidance understood this sleeping man's situation and guessed that he was the son of the lady who passed away recently. It is common that people need more help and support at the time of loss. Therefore, one can find many instances where people sleep and spend more time in the mosques and temples when they are spiritually troubled and in need. In this story, the Sufi handled the case with wisdom without confronting the harsh administrator directly, but addressed the problem to the general audience. This was one of the ways Rasulullah ﷺ used to solve any problem and issue among people. Rasulullah ﷺ did not target any specific person and accuse them of their mistakes but tried to teach them with the habit of introducing general guidelines for everyone.[38]

Discussion Question

- ► Why do people tend to have increased quality and quantity of spirituality at the time of loss?

56.   Warm Water in the Morning

There was a Sufi who liked coffee a lot; however, she started her day by drinking warm water rather than drinking coffee. One night, a friend of hers stayed overnight with the Sufi. Her friend knew that the Sufi loved coffee. She wanted to surprise her with a nice brewed pot of coffee in the morning when they woke up. The Sufi realized this and mindful of her friend's feelings she said, "I really love coffee but I need to train my body, stomach, and organs about what will come later in the day. Therefore, I start with warm water in the beginning then increase its strength by adding small amounts of coffee as time passes during the day."

IN PRACTICE

It is important to realize the stages of training and learning. The spiritual journey requires self-struggle constantly. The spiritual achievements come with self-increments. In the above story, the Sufi was implementing this notion in her everyday affairs even in her habit of drinking coffee.

Discussion Questions

- ▶ Can you give examples from the spiritual trainings of teachers for their disciples who implement the notion of incremental progress in the spiritual journey?
- ▶ How one can relate this concept with the early followers of Prophet Muhammad in Makkah compared to Madinah?
- ▶ How can one implement the notion of incremental progress in their spiritual journey?

57. Imbibing Patience

There was a Sufi who used to lose her temper. Each time she lost her temper she used to regret and blame herself about not being patient. She suffered pain after each incident of impatience. One day, she said to herself, "I don't know what to do." Then she started reading the Qurān and reviewed all the verses about patience. After, she was once again convinced logically that she should not lose her temper. Then, she felt better and promised to herself that she would be more mindful in applying patience.

IN PRACTICE

To imbibe patience is very important. It is a continuous struggle to embody the true meaning of patience. One of the ways to implement patience is with prayer. Another way is constantly being mindful that seemingly evil occurrences can be a gain if one is patient. This notion is constantly advised in the Qurān. Allah ﷻ is with the one who is patient. Allah ﷻ is the supporter of the patient one. A person should always rely on Allah ﷻ in the instances that require patience. Patience can be applied when facing evils. Patience can be applied for being on the right path. Patience can be applied for the struggles against one's own self if it encourages the person to do evil. If a person starts complaining and blames others, then at this stage there is no patience.[20] This is the stage where the blame comes in the relationship with Allah ﷻ. The relationship becomes shaky and unfruitful. Therefore, the Sufis practice chanting *Alhamdullilah* to appreciate Allah ﷻ. In the instances where utmost patience is needed they chant, *hasbiyallah*, Allah ﷻ is sufficient for me.

Discussion Questions

- ▸ Is it difficult to implement the notion of patience?
- ▸ Why is patience a virtue in many spiritual and religious traditions?

58. The Pain and the Pleasure

Each time after a painful ritual such as fasting, the Sufi used to feel good and strong for at least a week. However, before each optional fasting, she was always hesitant if she should fast that day or not. If for any reason she did not fast that day she did not feel well and got a headache. If she fasted she sometimes got a headache and she thought that her headache was related to her fasting.

IN PRACTICE

Fasting is one of the practices that focuses a person's mind and heart. It is also one of the ways of removing depression, stress, and anxiety. It is recommended to fast three days per month or one day per week as an optional practice. Mondays and Thursdays or the mid three days of the month are especially chosen for fasting as practiced by the Prophet.[20] In the story above, the Sufi received the benefit of fasting for at least a week although it was difficult for her.

Discussion Questions

- ► How can or cannot fasting trigger headaches?
- ► Why is fasting medically recommended if fasting can trigger headaches?
- ► What was the wisdom of Rasulullah ﷺ about getting headaches? Can headaches be related to fasting or other reasons?

59. The Focused Sufi

One day, the Sufi was in the mosque. Two people started arguing about a religious matter. The Sufi said to himself "I won't get involved." He tried to focus on his prayer. Finally, the arguing people left. The Sufi said, "*Alhamdulillah*, thanks to Allah ﷻ." A few minutes later, a crazy man came to the mosque. He started shaking people's hands and disturbing people while they were praying. The Sufi said to himself, "Maybe, this is a sign. Let me go to my car and finish my prayer and meditation over there." He went to his car and continued his meditation. After a while, he went to back into the mosque. Everything looked and felt peaceful and calm once again. Then, the Sufi serenely finished his meditation and said "*Alhamdulillah*, thanks to Allah ﷻ."

IN PRACTICE

Full focus during the prayer and meditation is very important. These are valuable times for a person to discharge and charge oneself spiritually. Sometimes, if the conditions are not amenable it is important to find other possible places to focus. Most of the time, mosques are places in which people can find tranquility, calmness, and peace for prayers. But there are always exceptions to the general rule. When there is the possibility of disturbance or evil outcomes, a person can leave the mosque until the negativity is gone then he or she can go back.

Discussion Question

- ▶ How can the spiritual medium of a place change in the case of argumentation or dispute among people?

60.   An Argument at the Mosque

One day, there were two people arguing in the mosque. One was an Arab and the other was an Indian. The Arab said, "We should follow the Prophet." The Indian said, "No, that is *sunnah muakkadah*." The Sufi looked at them both, smiling, and said to himself, "They are both saying the same thing but using different language of terminology. That is the main problem in our world."

IN PRACTICE

It is really important to have wisdom of understanding of people with their cultural, ethnic, and gender background. In the above story, two people from the same religion are arguing about a religious matter. They mean the same but because they use different words they think they disagree and argue. In the case of the Arab fellow in the story, he feels that he is qualified to directly access the primary sources related to the practice of the Prophet[12] by quoting Rasulullah ﷺ on a religious matter. Whereas the fellow from India follows his teacher and uses a technical term from his school of thought.[13] The Arab fellow does not know this technical term, and thinks the other one doesn't know anything. The Indian fellow does not know the source of the quote from Rasulullah ﷺ quoted by the other fellow, and thinks the other one equally ignorant.

Discussion Question

  ▶   Is it common to witness people arguing about an issue but they really mean something similar or the same? Why?

---

12. Hadith.
13. Hanifi school of Islamic legal system.

61. The Sufi, the Semi-Buddhist Sufi, and the Teachers

One day, there was a Sufi and semi-Buddhist Sufi and they were good friends. The semi-Buddhist Sufi also had teachers from the Buddhist tradition. They argued about whose teacher was better than the others.

IN PRACTICE

A wise Sufi tries to avoid religious arguments about the superiority of one's teachers over another. It is always important to respect other traditions if someone is identifying or viewing themselves as "semi" as in the story above. Semi is a term borrowed from physics when the nomenclature is used for example for semi-conductors, half or partial conducting metals. Semi in this case can mean a person following half of the teachings of one path and following the rest from another spiritual path. The arguments of identity chaining the person to specific teachers or schools is not new, unfortunately, along the history of practice. Genuine Sufis are not trapped in these futile arguments although one can view her or his teacher as the best and the most valuable. As one Sufi teacher said, "One can claim that his or her teacher or school is the best but one cannot claim that theirs is the only way."

Discussion Questions

- ▸ How can one define the concept of "semi" in one's life?
- ▸ Do you encounter people often who see or define themselves as "semi"?
- ▸ What is the advantage and disadvantage of being "semi"?

62.   The MP3 Player and the Corpse

Once there was a Sufi alone in the mosque, enjoying reading the Qurān, praying, and reflecting on the verses. After some time, a group of people entered the mosque with a dead body for funeral preparations for the next day. The Sufi still tried to enjoy his reading of the Qurān and praying but at the same heard some crying of the family members in the back bemoaning their loss. After half an hour, the family members left the body with a Qurān MP3 player in the washroom next to the prayer area. There was no one in the mosque again except the Sufi and the dead body in the washroom with the Qurān playing in the background. After the Sufi finished his prayer, he smiled and said to himself, "This is life. If I don't read the Qurān when I am alive, then what is the benefit of listening to it from MP3 when I am dead? The people leave and once again you are with the Beloved."

IN PRACTICE

Death is reality but not a bad one if the person internalizes it through practice and worship before it happens. In the above story, the Sufi underlines the real connection with the Qurān when one is alive. An unnatural or weak connection can be made when one is dead as well but not as much. People read the Qurān to the deceased for comforting and easing the travel from our life to the next.[44]

Discussion Questions

- ► How does recitation of the Qurān or divine phrases affect the death or the soul of the deceased?
- ► What are the common practices of prayers or recitations when one visits a grave? Why?

63.   The Patient Sufi

One Friday the Sufi was in the mosque enjoying his praying and reading the Qurãn. There were also three talkative men in the mosque. Others in the mosque treated them poorly, but the Sufi treated them gently and kindly. They knew and liked the Sufi and wished to consult him, but they also knew that they should not disturb him while he was reading the Qurãn or during prayers. One of the men needed the Sufi's attention and sat next to the Sufi. In general, the Sufi would not let himself be distracted while reading the Qurãn, but on this day he responded patiently. The man happily returned to his spot in the mosque. When the other two saw how the Sufi responded, they were encouraged as well and went next to the Sufi one by one. The Sufi responded kindly, thinking to himself, "Today is a special day, Friday. I am practicing patience."

In practice

If a person is enjoying a nice sweet dessert, he or she may not want to be disturbed.[45] For some senior Sufis, one's relationship with Allah ﷻ in the prayers and reading the Qurãn can have the same sweet taste. In the above story, the Sufi had that experience with the prayers and reading the Qurãn; however, he understood the desire for the three man to talk to him and entertained their conversations. The Sufi also realized that he should still continue his engagement with the prayer and reading the scripture after the disturbance by practicing genuine patience.

Discussion Questions

- ▶ Is it considered inconsiderate if one does not respond to one's need due to the person's sweet engagement in prayer or worship of Allah ﷻ? Why?
- ▶ Is it difficult to achieve the level of taking pleasure or sweetness from one's prayers?

64.   The Sunset, the Nice Breeze, and the Sufi

One day, the Sufi was sitting in the mosque. She was enjoying the sunset, the prayer, and the nice breeze from outside. She looked back upon some old memories from when she was a child. She felt that she had wasted all her life without Allah and said to herself, "I wish I knew then what I know now."

In practice

One of the ways to test the upward spiritual journey is that the person does not desire to go back to the living conditions of the past. In other words, the person constantly learns and increases one's knowledge in their relationship with Allah ﷻ. Every next day is better in that relationship than the one before. In that perspective, a person ideally is expected not to miss the past due to climbing upward spiritually. However, it is normal to miss old friends, places, and good experiences. [46]

Discussion Question

  ► How can one use the negative effect of past feelings positively in the present?

65. Submission, Decision, and the Sufis

There were two Sufis: husband and wife. They were trying to decide which teacher they should send their children to for their self and spiritual training. The wife said, "Let's decide and get it over with." The husband said, "I am not sure really which one is better." They discussed and talked without reaching a solution and until both were tired. After a few hours, the wife received a text from one of the potential teachers of the child saying, "I am sick; please don't send your child." The husband said, "*Alhamdulillah*, the decision is made."

IN PRACTICE

In choosing what they want for themselves, for their families, and others, there are times when people use logic and their minds to make the best life decisions. One of the main concepts in practice is the concept of positive and active submission and surrender to Allah ﷻ. One may call this as reliance or *tawakkul*. It is a positive submission and surrender to Allah ﷻ because the person does not see the relationship between Allah ﷻ and oneself as something negative and passive submission to an authority. The One Who is Caring, Merciful, and at the same time the Most Powerful and Wise can do anything for the person if the person submits and surrenders. This notion takes all the burden of worries, stress, and unnecessary load from the spiritual shoulders of a person. The above story is a small example of this in practice. The concept of submission or reliance can reveal itself explicitly as in the above case. In other cases, it may be implicit, so a person should know the etiquettes of the path to reach this level and apply it with patience in different parts of life.

Discussion Questions

- ▸ Why is it so difficult to make decisions for some people?
- ▸ What is the balance between indecisiveness and decisiveness in an ideal spiritual path?

66. Blessing the Coffee

There was once a class with a Sufi and his teacher who was also a famous coffee maker. The teacher often made coffee for the students before class. The Sufi asked if the teacher could teach the Sufi how to make the coffee. The teacher said, "OK, first you say '*bismillah*,' with the name of Allah ﷻ, then put in the filter and water with your right hand. It is important to use a natural filter and make the coffee light. Put seven small spoonfuls of coffee in the filter while saying *bismillah*. Enjoy its aroma while it brews, and serve it as soon as it is done so that it doesn't get bitter. This is the recipe of my famous coffee."

In practice

It is important to chant on the food and drink to get a blessing from Allah ﷻ. The chanting is the recognition of the blessing of Allah ﷻ.[47] According to some Sufis, it tastes better when chanted on. It is the practice of Rasulullah ﷺ to use odd numbers such as 1, 3, 5, or as mentioned 7 for the number of spoonfuls of coffee. Sufis are careful to choose an organic coffee filter and use natural and organic ingredients[14] as suggested by the Qurãn. There is actually an entire market for the practice of herbal and healthy and prophetic food habits and medicine.

Sufis adjust their qualities and tones to benefit everyone without leaving people out of the circle. Strong coffee only appeals to the specialized drinker. Therefore, making the coffee light can increase its accessibility to even those not commonly coffee drinkers. It is important to maximize the tastes as the teacher suggests by drinking as soon as it's brewed, and savoring the smell of the coffee while brewing and before drinking it. This notion alludes to the practice of mindfulness and awareness while being engaged in chants or other everyday affairs.

Discussion Question

 ▶ How does one's chanting over a food possibly affect the taste of it?

---

14. Tayyib.

67. Accountability, Children, and the Sufi

One day, the wife of the Sufi listed all the bad things that their children did. The children were not listening to their mother. The mother felt helpless. The Sufi said to himself, "If I discipline them, I would be seen as harsh. I won't do anything and will just be silent and watch what happens." Days passed, and the mother became uneasy about the children's abuse, and started to lose control of herself. The house was becoming a chaotic environment. The Sufi said to himself, "I think I need to do something. Let me act firmly." The Sufi called the children and listed all the blames that were reported by the mother. There was silence from the children. The Sufi declared, "One of you needs to sleep upstairs and the other downstairs. You will not sleep in your beds tonight because of what has been happening lately." One went upstairs and the other went downstairs and both children burst out crying. The mother was uneasy, her heart broken. She tried to talk to their father into removing the punishment. The Sufi remained firm, thinking, "*SubhanAllah*, this is similar to people and their relationship with Allah ﷻ."

IN PRACTICE

It is important to realize that there is an accountability in this world and afterlife. People are at different levels in their ethics and spirituality. Some people may not do evil because they are afraid of its consequence. Others may not do evil because it is not right for them ethically or spiritually. The accountability in the afterlife is necessary for both the affairs of spiritual and worldly engagements. Most elect the spiritual path of performing good actions to avoid evils as classified by Allah ﷻ in order to not displease Allah ﷻ. They avoid evil because they love Allah ﷻ. On the other hand, the lower level travelers, with no blame to them, can perform good and avoid evil due to fear of accountability and the desire for reward. All are good and fine.[22]

Discussion Question

▸   What can be the problems of humanization of the Divine realities in the above case?

68. Terminology of Jealousy

The Sufi one day went to an interfaith meeting. There were Christians and Muslims, and they were talking about Allah ﷻ. The Christian fellow said, "We believe that our Allah ﷻ is jealous." The Muslim fellow said, "Allah does not want anyone to be worshipped except Allah." They continued debating. The Sufi looked and smiled and said to himself, "Our Creator is the same. They both say the same thing but in different words and terminologies."

IN PRACTICE

It is very important to worship only Allah ﷻ. It is very important to keep proper etiquette and respectful attitude toward Allah ﷻ[15] when one is expressing words and even thinking about Allah ﷻ. This may be called *adab* with Allah ﷻ. Therefore, although what is implied with "jealous" is understood when one is using this word about Allah ﷻ, but it can also be alienating due to popular human use of this word in negative contexts. [26] One of the parts that Sufis focus upon in their practice is to change terminologies for people in order to approximate them with what they mean all the while with a consideration of keeping the attitude of respect, appreciation, and a humble attitude toward Allah ﷻ.

Discussion Questions

- ▶ Why do we have different classifications of relationships with others depending on the people and context such as professional, socia, and family relations?
- ▶ How does one expect an appropriate relationship with Allah ﷻ similar to the case of different classifications of relationships in a person's life? Why?

---

15. Adab.

69.   The Overflowing Cup

One day, the Sufi poured coffee into a small cup, trying to get in as much as possible. It spilled on his hand, scalding him. He said to himself, "I was greedy. I wanted to get more than I can handle. I got burned."

IN PRACTICE

Allah ﷻ gives people what they can handle or what they can bear with tests, trials, and spiritual achievements. When a person wants to achieve more, sometimes it could be difficult and can possibly backfire upon him or herself. Therefore, the person should be always in the mode of appreciation of Allah ﷻ for the all of life's encounters.

Discussion Question

> ▸   Is having limits as humans a blessing or not? Why?

70. Advising Patience, Real Patience, and the Sufi

There was a nice Sufi who used to advise people to be patient. One day, he heard such shocking news about himself that it changed his life. He said to himself, "I now understand it is not easy to be patient." He smiled sadly and felt the pain of the deep change in his life.

IN PRACTICE

It is really not easy to implement the teachings. "Easier said than done" is a good expression to show the notion of the embodiment of patience. When a person loses their loved ones, job, or other things to which the person is attached, it is difficult to implement the notion of patience. The trials and tests attack the person from their attachments. The constant expression of *"La ilaha illa Allah"* removes the attachments from a person's heart and mind.[22]

Discussion Questions

- ▸ Why is it difficult to implement patience?
- ▸ Is the trait of patience earned or given at birth? Why?

71. Life Vests

One day, the Sufi witnessed an evil-seeming incident. The pain of the evil remained with her for days. The Sufi constantly asked the question to herself, "Why, why, why . . ." At the same, the Sufi asked Allah ﷻ to make it easy during this painful period of grief. She said to herself, "It is a dead end. I need to move on."

IN PRACTICE

Sometimes endless reasoning self-conversations can drown a person in pessimism. It is important to ask Allah ﷻ to ease the pain of a person during times of evil. The person should continue their day-to-day practices. These practices can act as life vests to save a person from pain. Therefore, the person can activate the belief of destiny with submission and surrender and move on as mentioned in the above story.

Discussion Question

- ▸ What should be the balance between self-accountability and excessive questioning of oneself leading to pessimism?

72. Bad News

The Sufi was living her life regularly with not much change. She enjoyed the prayers and reading the signs of Allah ﷻ every day in nature and in the Qurān. One day, she got news of a loss that she expected would affect her entire life. She felt pain, but then she thought about similar experiences in her life. After each change, there was something good and even better than before, but she needed to be patient. She said, "OK, I know: I plan and Allah plans. I just need to submit and surrender myself and ask for the good outcome of this change from Allah." She also realized that she was becoming older and remembered death and said to herself, "*Alhamdullillah*, I will meet with Allah soon. I hope all the changes are good that will ultimately benefit me *inshAllah* in this meeting."

IN PRACTICE

Expect the unexpected. Initially it can be painful, but ultimately a person can treat their pain with prayer, reading the Qurān and understanding and personalizing it. In these unknowns and the unexpected, one should always try the easy and natural way: submission and surrender and trust in Allah ﷻ, Allah. On the other hand, complaining, not submitting or surrendering will produce friction as in the laws of conservation of energy in physics. It will cause the person to lose energy unnecessarily. Another powerful way of coping with any type of grief is embracing the concept of death. When a person knows that this life is short and they will meet with the Lover—Allah ﷻ—soon with all the struggles on the Divine path, then the person can also feel relief from grief as well.

Discussion Questions

- ▸ Why are unexpected news often not welcomed?
- ▸ What makes a news expected or unexpected?
- ▸ Can a person develop a skill to cope with the concept of dealing with different types of news? How can this be related to one's relationship with Allah ﷻ?

73. Circular Days

There was a Sufi who tried to understand the meanings in people's lives. She realized that sometimes people are hit with evil and become sad. Sometimes, they are so happy because of their achievements. Sometimes, they seem neutral. The Sufi said to herself: "This is like a circle. It goes and comes back again."

IN PRACTICE

Understand that Allah ﷻ changes the conditions of people throughout life. The Qurãn uses an expression as "rotating the days among people." In this perspective, a possible piece of wisdom in the change of the conditions of people is to evaluate whether they will maintain the state of appreciation of Allah ﷻ in good, evil, and neutral times. Therefore, one of the goals in the spiritual journey is not to change the level of positive appreciation for Allah ﷻ in all conditions: adversity, joy, and neutrality.[48]

Discussion Question

> ▸ How can a person welcome and appreciate an evil-seeming incident?

74. The Religious Laws, the Spiritual Discoveries, and the Sufi

One day, the Sufi was thinking about the benefits of fasting. Then, she deduced from her spiritual discovery that Monday fasting prevents sicknesses and Thursday fasting prevents evils in one's life. The Sufi used to be sick on Mondays when she did not fast and she used to get bad news on Thursdays when she did not fast. One day, the Sufi fasted on a Monday but still got sick and she said to herself, "Either my discovery has an exception or it is wrong."

IN PRACTICE

Religious laws are there for everyone. They put the boundaries of limits with logic and they should be objective. If a person does not follow a religious guideline or a religious law, then he or she will be held responsible in front of Allah ﷻ.[48] Conversely, spiritual discoveries can be sometimes right or wrong as well as personal and subjective. There is no requirement for it, but if a person follows these discoveries, they may receive spiritual "cookies" in this world and afterlife. Although there is always wisdom in following religious laws or guidelines, a person does it or performs it because Allah ﷻ says so. This wisdom can be sometimes known or unknown to the person. The person intends not to do it due to its benefits but to please Allah ﷻ. Alternatively, the Sufis also try to practice with this intention. In addition, they tap into the possible wisdom of a practice and extend it to their lives with some personal embodiment of these rituals.

Discussion Questions

- ► What makes religious laws more dependable than religious personal experiences?
- ► Why are clear and simple religious and spiritual guidelines important?

75. The Hailstorm

There once was a Sufi who had a very special relationship with Allah ﷻ. One day, she got hit in her life with something evil. She thought about what she should do. First, she prayed to Allah ﷻ. Second, she wondered what the next step she should take should be. Although the effect of the evil was painful for her, she tried to be patient. She said to herself, "OK, I need to ask the opinion of at least three people who love me and are willing to help me in dealing with this evil." She opened up to her first friend, but while she spoke she felt uncomfortable about it and immediately a hail shower started outside. She contemplated the meaning of the hail as she went to her second friend to discuss her problem. She started the topic and again felt pained sharing her problem with a person other than Allah ﷻ. Again, a hail shower started outside and she thought about the meaning of the hail. She started praying and afterward smiled and said to herself, "Hail means Allah ﷻ does not want me to open my problem to anyone. Allah ﷻ is sufficient for me! What a nice Friend! What a nice Supporter!"

IN PRACTICE

There are different levels in one's relationship with Allah ﷻ. In normative practice, it is encouraged to discuss one's problems with the experts of the field who have concern for others. But for some high level elect mystics and Sufis, opening one's problem to someone other than Allah ﷻ is a disrespectful attitude to Allah ﷻ. In other words, Allah ﷻ is the Best Supporter and Friend for the person. In the above story, the Sufi interpreted the hard hail shower from nowhere in each instance as a sign that her close relationship with Allah ﷻ required only taking Allah ﷻ as the real and the Best Friend and Supporter in all types of evil encounters of life. As the teaching of Rasulullah ﷺ Muhammad, one of the expressions chanted every day seven times in the morning and at night is the expression of "Hasbiya Allah La ilaha illa Hu Alayhi Tawwakaltu wa Huwa Rabbul Arshil Azim," which means Allah ﷻ is Sufficient for me, there is no deity except Allah ﷻ, I rely on Allah ﷻ and Allah ﷻ is the Most Exalted High Holder of Authority and Dominance.[42]

Discussion Question

- How can a person develop secrecy and privacy[xiiviii] with Allah ﷻ?

76. The Daily Deception

As the Sufi woke up every day, she felt energetic, powerful, and hopeful. When she went to bed, she felt very pessimistic, fearful, and weak. One day, she thought during the time of midday: What is the balance? What is real? What is deception? Then, she heard that someone died and there would be a funeral in the mosque. She said to herself: "Now I understand; this is the reality."

IN PRACTICE

Life is limited. Every day, hope is good to keep a person going as long as it is balanced with the reality of death. In other words, one of the spiritual diseases that most people fall into is the notion or deception of living as if the person is not going to die. The reality of death gives the person the checks and balances for this life and the afterlife. On the other hand, a person who is in self-deception of not dying can be hit hard with death or an evil, leading to death if she or he does not actualize this reality. Some Sufi scholars think that most of the painful detachments of life are due to this disease of lack of considering and reflection on death and dying.[16]

Discussion Questions

- ► Can thinking about death make a person depressive and pessimistic? Why?
- ► Why is it suggested to think about the reality of death?

---

16. This disease is called *"tulu-amal"* in Sufi terminology.

77. Joking in Company

One day, the Sufi attended an interfaith gathering. There were some discussions about teachers and their level of piety as they are the role models for humans. One of the attendees started explaining one of the teachers' parents' ethical behavior and how parents affect their children. The Sufi made a joke about the story, and everyone started laughing. The Sufi paused for a minute, horrified. He said to himself, "What did I do? Shame on me!"

IN PRACTICE

Respect beliefs, values, elders, and teachers. Although we are living in a society of jokes, the Sufis believe that jokes have limits and should not touch upon sacred items. According to the Sufis, the religion, the belief, and the practice is all attitude, *adab*. In other words, the state of being with Allah ﷻ and friendship with Allah ﷻ requires maintenance of proper respect and *adab*. Most of the time, people lose their good friends due to overstepping boundaries. In this case, having respectful boundaries with the sacred—the Qurān, teachers, and Allah ﷻ—is the key for successful and a regular spiritual journey until one dies.

Discussion Questions

- What should be the balance among the topics selected for joking or fun?
- Can religious topics be risky as topics of making jokes or fun? Why?

78. Learning, Questions, and Patience

One day, the Sufi was teaching the importance of patience in asking questions while learning. She did not talk to the students and maintained silence. The students were trying to ask questions. The Sufi smiled and continued reading her book. After a while, the students kept reading their books as well when they saw that their teacher was reading. The Sufi then said to herself, "Most of the time, if we learn patience before asking questions, the answers will be given in a sweet way."

IN PRACTICE

It is important to wait for the answer to a question until there is a good time and place for it. A wrong question at a wrong time and place can make the person deduce wrong meanings. This can alienate the person from genuine learning. One of the genuine ways of learning is to be with a teacher and learn and observe natural discourse, occurring events, and deduce meaning. There are a lot of times that a teacher can formally answer people's questions for them to learn as well.

Discussion Questions

- ► How do you understand the above teaching about asking questions especially at our times of encouragement for inquiry?
- ► Do you learn better when you ask a question, or when you observe and deduce the answers by reflection and spiritual experience?

79.   Memories, Pain, the Reality of Missing, and the Sufi

The Sufi used to think about all her past nice memories. She felt much pain longing for them: her old friends, mother, father, brothers, sisters, and cherished places. One day, the Sufi again remembered all these nice memories. But now she did not feel pain of longing. She thought and said to herself: "Everything that I miss is temporary. I give them a value as if they are permanent and can benefit me. I think I just miss Allah ﷻ who is my Friend regardless of time and place."

In practice

It is normal to be saddened by memories, especially of missed good teachers, parents, and friends. But all memories and created beings have limits. Putting too much value on them can be painful and result in not giving the full due to the One who deserves to be missed limitlessly. Compared to all other missed items, Allah ﷻ knows and appreciates a person's missing and burning feelings for union with Allah ﷻ.[49] These emotions, feelings, thoughts, instances, minutes, or days can elevate the person in front of Allah ﷻ vertically. This person can be rewarded immensely in this world and in the afterlife by Allah ﷻ.

Discussion Question

- ▸ How can one minimize the effects of pain due to the detachment from loved ones?

80. The Difficulty of Being Human

One day, the Sufi was thinking about how difficult it was to be a human. The Sufi thought to herself: "I should not break anyone's heart. I should be nice. I should be fair. I should not be angry. I should not be jealous. I should truly appreciate Allah ﷻ." As she was thinking about all of that she said to herself "*Alhamdulillah*, I am trying *inshAllah*."

IN PRACTICE

It is difficult to be a true human being. Everyone can claim that they possess human qualities, but in practice that is not always the case. The statements by the Sufi are some of the expected traits of a person on the path: not breaking people's hearts because Allah ﷻ is with the broken hearts; being fair even if it is against your own interests; using anger to fight injustice not for oppression. The most difficult part is not truly appreciating Allah ﷻ. But, in the end, Allah ﷻ appreciates all the efforts but not the results. Therefore, the Sufi says, "*Alhamdullilah*, all thanks and gratitude belongs to Allah ﷻ for I am trying."

Discussion Question

▶   Why is trying or struggle one of the most important notions in practice?

81. Fears, Belief, and the Sufi

One day, the Sufi was thinking about why she was fearful every day: afraid of people, afraid of the unknown, fearful of death, and so forth. She chanted the divine phrases but she was still fearful. She said to herself, "I should pray to Allah ﷻ to embody these phrases in my life."

IN PRACTICE

Life and practice are a struggle. The person is expected only to take refuge in Allah in all the circumstances of fearful instances. Although one may still have the traces of fear from others, it is important to aim to remove this fear with practice, prayer, and through struggle. Although the Sufi was practicing the divine phrases and chanting them, she still carried the feeling of fear in daily discourses and encounters. She concluded that she needs to embody the removal of fear from everything except Allah ﷻ, through "*La ilaha illa Allah.*" There is nothing to be fearful of except not taking refuge in Allah ﷻ.

Discussion Questions

- ▶ What makes humans different than the angels in practice?
- ▶ How can one relate the schmooze of Satan with Adam in Heaven in the context of manipulating Adam to be perfect like the angels?17

---

17. One can review the Qurãn [7:20–21] about this incident.

82. Flies, Friends, and Life

One day, the Sufi was reading a book on a cold day in the mosque. There was no one except a small fly flying around the Sufi. The Sufi said to the fly "*SubhanAllah*, on a cold winter day, it is amazing to see a fly. Everything outside is dead because of the snow. How beautiful is life! How beautiful is *Al-Hayy*! How beautiful is my friend, the fly!"

IN PRACTICE

Anything with life reminds one of Allah ﷻ. Anything with life is a sign from Allah ﷻ. One of the names of Allah ﷻ is *Al-Hayy*, the Source and the Creator of Life. Some people chant this phrase in times of depression and anxiety in order to relax and to receive positive energy from Allah ﷻ. There are a lot of Sufi stories about being friends with animals. It is not common in the history of this genuine practice that people have been imprisoned by others when they preached all inclusive, loving, and respect requesting motifs for Allah ﷻ. Therefore, it is not uncommon to encounter stories of imprisoned Sufi where the Sufis are friends even with some of the disliked animals for most humans such as flies, snakes, or mice. The Sufis view them as not something to be disliked but as holders of life, reminding of their Creator, *Al-Hayy*. They are signs from Allah ﷻ if one can understand their meaning and purpose.

Discussion Question

► Why do people tend to be happy when they see a living being in a deserted area even though this living being can be something or someone disliked in normal conditions?

83. The Unemployed Sufi and Reliance to Allah ﷻ

There was a Sufi who had a very personal and close relationship with Allah ﷻ. Whatever she asked from Allah ﷻ, Allah ﷻ gave her exactly what she wanted. One day, she lost her job. She was afraid that if she asked Allah ﷻ, Allah ﷻ would give her what she exactly wanted. Then, she said to herself "I will make *tawakkul* and show reliance to Allah ﷻ and pray for whatever Allah ﷻ chooses to give for me. I am happy as long as Allah ﷻ is pleased with me. "

In practice

It is important to reach the level of reliance, *tawakkul* in practice. Most of the time when evil happens we tend to blame people or Allah ﷻ and ruin our relationships. In the above story, the Sufi had a very close relationship with Allah ﷻ through constant prayer and appreciation. Therefore, Allah ﷻ gave her always what she wanted in life. The Sufi reached one of the highest levels of reliance called *tawakkul*. In this stage, all the evil or good-looking incidents are the same for the person as long as Allah ﷻ is pleased with that person.

Discussion Question

- ▶ Is it easy or difficult to make reliance or tawakkul? Why?

84.   Benefit of the Doubt for the Deaf Man

There was a deaf man for whom the Sufi felt much compassion. He asked what he could do as work in order to help him. The deaf man mentioned that he could do some cleaning for the Sufi, and the Sufi accepted. The deaf person did not show up on the promised day. They agreed for another day. He did not show up again. They agreed again for a third time. The deaf man did not show up again. The Sufi thought to himself, "I am not going to think that he did not fulfill his promise. I will still make a good excuse for him."

In Practice

Allah ﷻ knows the inside and out of all things. As humans, we try to help people with our best intention. In the above story, the Sufi did not want to think badly of the deaf man. It is important to make or generate good excuses in one's mind in order not to blame people for their faults. This is called *husnu zann*, thinking always good about others. The opposite of this is called *su-i zann*, thinking and assuming always bad about others. The person is always encouraged to practice *husnu zann* and not the opposite.

Discussion Question

- ► What is the benefit of thinking always good about others?

85.   Emotions, Mind, Disputes, and the Sufi

One morning, the Sufi was in dispute with his wife. He said to himself, "If I use my mind, I will not burst out with my anger and not discharge myself. I will be better later but not now. If I use my emotions, I will explode and discharge myself. I will feel good now but will regret and feel terrible later. What should I do?" He was unable to help himself and used his emotions and burst out with his anger, but by midday regretted his choice and said to himself, "I wish I had used my mind."

IN PRACTICE

It is important to use one's mind when emotions and mind are in conflict. Emotions are not always called heart or conscience. The true emotions or inspirations coming from the heart or conscience do not conflict with the mind, logic, and reason. If they are conflicting, then these emotions can be self- or Satan-generated sources that can lead to evil. At times of conflict, disputes, and anger, these emotions or thoughts can overpower a person's mind, heart, and conscience. One should make their best effort not to be trapped in these temptations in order not to say "I wish" later.

Discussion Questions

- ► Why do we tend to follow our emotions although we know that it is wrong to do so?
- ► In which cases are there benefits or harms of saying "I wish"?

86.   Disputes, the Sufi, and Moving On

One day, the Sufi was in conflict with her husband, and for a few days afterwards her husband was still angry with her. He took the dispute personally and carried his anger. The Sufi thought, "I should not take it personally but move on." A few days later, everything seemed normal. The Sufi said: "*Alhamdulillah*, thanks and all appreciation belongs to Allah SWT."

IN PRACTICE

It is important not to take things personally and expand the conflict more among people, especially between spouses. This notion is much embedded in the Qurãn as a suggested way of "moving on with peace": not taking things too personally in disputes. There are many stories about rulers in Islamic history whose spouses used to freely criticize and yell at them. These rulers wisely observed silence and patience, especially in family relations.

Discussion Question

- ► In which cases are there benefits or harms from taking things personally?

87. The Cancer of Arrogance

There was a man who used to always criticize the concept of surrender and submission. He used to always try to rationalize everything. The Sufi used to try to explain to him the importance of submission and surrender to Allah ﷻ as well as the importance of reason. The man got offended and used to say, "This is why we need enlightenment. Religion always puts us in darkness. We need to rationalize everything." One day, this person got sick. His illness continued for a month, a year, and then two years. Doctors finally diagnosed him with a rare type of cancer. The Sufi was saddened by the news. The devastated man came to the Sufi and said, "Now, I know what you mean. I need to pray to Allah ﷻ and submit myself to the All Powerful One."

IN PRACTICE

Belief is an attitude, and an attitude of humility can elevate a person. Sometimes different life experiences can make a person angry with everything and even alienate them from Allah ﷻ due to frustration and anger. It is important to always remind oneself of the weaknesses, needs, and fragility of humans. Constant prayers and chants with their meanings charge the person with power by connecting him or herself to the source of All Power, Allah ﷻ.

Discussion Questions

- ▸ How can one understand the concept of submission in one's relation with other humans?
- ▸ How can one understand the concept of submission in one's relation with Allah ﷻ?
- ▸ What is the relationship between submission and arrogance?

88. Distractions and Focus

One day the Sufi was thinking about the purpose of life, its distractions, and the peace found with focusing on Allah. Then, he remembered two names of Allah, *Al-Wahid* and *Al-Ahad*. He said to himself, "This is the key: being with Allah everywhere at all times of distraction is *Al-Wahid* and being with Allah when you are alone and focusing on Allah which is *Al-Ahad*. This is the purpose. This is the trial. This is the difficulty."

In practice

It is important to be with Allah ﷻ always in one's virtual space of tranquility and calmness. *Al Wahid* means accepting Allah, the One, through all many creations. *Al-Ahad* is knowing Allah, the One and the Unique by focusing on one creation. Sometimes the distractions in life can make one heedless about Allah ﷻ. With constant effort and struggle, it is important to connect the name of *Al-Wahid* to Allah ﷻ.

Discussion Question

- How can one develop the habit of forming a virtual space of tranquility and calmness?

89.   The Bored Sufi and the Virtual Space

One day, the Sufi attended a meeting at her work. She was not interested much in the topic discussed but she was still trying to pay attention in order not to be disrespectful. She kept thinking what she should do in order to collect herself spiritually, not be bored, and how to enjoy her time and presence in that space. She said to herself "*dhikr.*" After a few minutes, she felt much better.

IN PRACTICE

It is important to recognize people's spiritual needs. Just as one may need to leave a meeting for a few minutes to go to a restroom, sometimes spiritual urges can come at different times so that a person may need a few minutes of break. In that respect, prayers regularly during the day five times can help a person minimize and structure these spiritual urges as they may pop up at any time and place. As in the case of the above story, a person sometimes may not need to leave the room or the physical space of presence. Rather, the person in a boring meeting can transform their state to a virtual space of peace and tranquility by reorienting and assuming himself or herself through a few seconds of remembrance of Allah ﷻ ("*dhikr*"). In this transformation, one can change any undesirable physical condition to a state of peace and ease through chants, prayer, and spiritual re-orientation.

Discussion Question

►   How can one's spiritual engagements affect the productivity of a person at a workplace?

90. Salawat, Remembering Teachers, and the Sufi

One day, the Sufi woke up feeling anxious and did not feel good. She asked herself what she should do. Then, she started making *salawat* and *tahiyyat* and immediately felt better.

IN PRACTICE

It is very critical to remember all the teachers, especially the main one, the Prophet. There are a lot of practices of chanting to remember Rasulullah ﷺ in different forms called *salawat* and *tahiyyat*. In some Sufi cultures the tradition is to get together, to sing, and to chant these phrases collectively. It is also customary to recite these chants daily in times of difficulty and sickness. The remembrance in the form of chants can bring blessings and ease in one's life.

Discussion Question

- ▶ How can remembering teachers and chanting on them (such as salawat) bring easiness and tranquility in one's spiritual state?

91. The Barber, the Beard, and the Accident

Once there was a Sufi who was very proud of his nice, long beard. He used to hold it when he was stressed. He used to look at the mirror and smile, proud that he was following the ways of the prophets by having a nice, long beard. One day, he went to a barber to trim some extra hair on his neck. This particular barber was a Sufi, always engaged with chanting and remembrance of the Divine phrases. During one of these moments, as he was trimming hairs on the Sufi's neck, he closed his eyes in his trance. By accident, he cut the beard of the Sufi. The Sufi screamed and cried, "My beard!" The barber jumped. He did not know what was happening. The Sufi who lost his beard smiled and said to himself, "My attachment to my beard."

IN PRACTICE

It is *Sunnah*, encouraged, and rewarding to follow the ways of the role models such as prophets. However, one should remember that doing so can cause arrogance and unhealthy attachment, and negate humility. In the above case, although the Sufi was proud of his beard, he understood that any attachment can be a test on the path of Allah ﷻ if it is not seen as a means to please Allah ﷻ. In other words, the only attachment one should have is to Allah ﷻ.

Discussion Question

- ▶ How can a person practice the religious guidelines and still see them as means but not the goal?

92. Learning with the Children

One day, the Sufi was studying with her children. She gave some studying materials to them. At first, the kids whined about the work. As they continued studying, they got excited about learning and discovering on their own the unknown realities. The Sufi as a teacher knew all the answers of the questions that she was trying to teach. As the lessons continued, she was amazed about the reaction of the kids and their self-satisfaction due to learning by struggle. The Sufi said to herself ,"If I gave the answers from the beginning they would not learn this well, and would not enjoy and appreciate the knowledge." The Sufi said to herself "*SubhanAllah*, this is similar to the tests, trials, and struggles to self-witness of one's actions and come closer to Allah ﷻ until one dies."

IN PRACTICE

It is important to realize that Allah knows everything, future and the past. One of the secrets of life is that Allah creates humans to self-witness their own journey in their relationship with Allah ﷻ. Thus, humans cannot claim otherwise in front of Allah ﷻ after death.

Discussion Question

- ▶ Why do people tend to appreciate their own effort of self-discoveries compared to outcomes or achievements given without much effort?

93. The Sufi's To-Do List

One morning, the Sufi woke up and was excited to start her prayers, read the Qurãn, and reflect on them. Then she remembered all the things that she needed to do that day, and she grew a little depressed, unhappy, and stressed. But she finished the nicest part of her day: the prayers and reading. Then, as she started the second part of her day, she said to herself, "I just need to do what needs to be done. If the things do not go in the way that I wanted, at least I tried within the reasons and means."

IN PRACTICE

It is important to follow the reasons and means through the faculties of the mind although one's heart or spiritual faculties may not feel engaged about it. These are the times where the mind should dominate the heart. When a person is used to being in a secluded life of prayers without socializing with people, they can feel secure due to the lack of human disturbances. Once a person starts interacting with others there are always possibilities of stress, broken hearts, oppression, and evil. Therefore, some Sufis prefer living in mountains in seclusion. But most Sufis find that this is not the way to go. It is better to live a social life and be with people, being patient to their vulgar treatments with the intention of teaching them while at the same time living in a virtual space of union with Allah ﷻ through prayers, chants, and reading the Divine Qurãn.

Discussion Question

- ▶ Is it possible to earn a peaceful state of mind and heart in both worldly and spiritual matters? Why?

94.   The Bugs, the Belief, and the Sufi

One day, there was food at the kitchen table. The mother put a cover on the food to protect it from the bugs. The Sufi saw it and said to himself, "Wow, this is similar to protecting one's *iman* (belief) from bugs when interacting with others."

IN PRACTICE

It is important to choose people of genuine knowledge and practice with whom to surround oneself. Once a person is with them the person should benefit through all means: presence, observation, and asking questions. If a person is with unauthentic people of knowledge and practice, one should be trained how to filter, what to learn, and what to block.

Discussion Question

> Why is it so emphasized to protect one's spiritual valuables?

95. Wishing for Coffee

One day, the Sufi was thinking of making a nice coffee for herself to enjoy. She started to think to herself, "I need to get up, put water in the coffee machine, put in the coffee and then I need to wait until it brews. It is too much work. I wish it just happened as I thought about it."

In Practice

According to the teachings in practice, patience and struggle are needed to achieve the worldly pleasures in this life. For example, if someone wants to travel for vacation, they take the challenge of difficulties of traveling and they need to be patient until they reach their destination. Therefore, if the person acquires the traits of being patient and applying self-struggle and uses it for noble purposes for this life and the afterlife, then Allah ﷻ promises in Heaven the pleasures without any self-struggle or patience. The pleasures in Heaven will appear in front of the person as the person thinks about them.

Discussion Question

> ► Why are the worldly or spiritual achievements or results linked to struggles?

96. Trials & Tests

The Sufi's best friend, the lamp, was stolen by envious individuals one day. The Sufi was so distressed and upset that he exclaimed, "This is the third time! By removing my lamp once more, they display a childish attitude. I do not comprehend these individuals. They come to pray and appear to be so devout, yet they commit evil in the mosque." The Sufi said, "I will leave it up to Allah ﷻ. I fear the punishment will not be so pleasant."

IN PRACTICE

One should anticipate tribulations and trials, but should continually pray to Allah ﷻ for protection against them. Even if a person does not cause harm to others, there will be those who attempt to annoy, harm, and sometimes abuse them. In these circumstances, it is essential to open yourself up to Allah ﷻ and then take the necessary steps. Sometimes, it is important to be patient and do nothing. Occasionally, a person may need to make some prudent decisions. Everything is context dependent.

Discussion Questions

- ▸ Discuss a time when you witnessed a conflict situation work itself out better without your interference. This may be because you intentionally restrained your emotional reaction or it may be because of circumstances beyond your control, the important thing is that, afterwards, you acknowledged to yourself that your interference would have complicated the issue.
- ▸ Discuss a time when you accidentally made a situation worse by interfering, even with good intentions. What caused you to take action? Was it fear, anger, or another emotion? A desire to control the situation, or something else?
- ▸ What is the value of exercising patience and wisdom in the appropriate context regarding improving one's relationships with other people?
- ▸ What is the value of exercising patience and wisdom regarding improving one's personal relationship with Allah ﷻ?

97. The Downtrodden

There was a man who frequently prayed in the mosque. Except for the Sufi, everyone viewed him as evil and unpleasant, and they were unwilling to interact with him. As suggested by the Prophet, Sufis enjoyed interacting with people who were considered outcasts or destitute.

IN PRACTICE

It is essential to interact with individuals who have low economic and social status in the society. Rasulullah ﷺ favored sitting among the poor and disadvantaged. He preferred to eat on the floor because slaves ate on the floor at the time, and he stated, "I am a slave of Allah ﷻ, so I eat on the floor." [1]

98. Knowledge and its Use

The Sufi was contemplating knowledge one day. She reflected, "There are numerous things to learn in life. Life is brief. What am I to learn? My lifetime is insufficient to acquire all knowledge." After which, she said, "Okay, I should acquire the knowledge that will be useful to me in this world and the afterlife so that I can apply it to my life now."

In practice

Unutilized or irrelevant learning or knowledge can be a source of distraction. The individual does not learn for his or her own sake. Understanding one's purpose in relation to the Qur'an constitutes the most essential knowledge. As a person gains knowledge, everything makes more sense, and he or she can increase the quality and quantity of his or her relationship with Allah ﷻ. This type of knowledge and participation benefits the individual both in this life and the next.

Discussion Questions

- ► What kind of knowledge is useful to you in your life?
- ► What knowledge do you personally find to be purposeless in your life?

99.   Ant and the Prayer

An ant appeared in the Sufi's hand as she was about to begin her daily protection, "*A'uzu bi kalimatillahi tammati min sharri ma khalaq*," one day. The Sufi exclaimed, "Wow! This is the power of prayer!"

IN PRACTICE

Prayers are the individual's weapons [50]. When a person takes full refuge in Allah ﷻ with the correct prayers as instructed by the Prophet, Allah ﷻ protects him or her. In the preceding narrative, the Sufi began reciting her daily protection prayer as instructed by the Prophet[ix]. As soon as the Sufi began the prayer, she noticed an ant on her body that she had not noticed before. This prayer means, "I take refuge in the full and perfect words of Allah ﷻ from the evil of Allah ﷻ's creation."

100. Displeasing Allah ﷻ

One day, the Sufi encountered a religious scholar and they began conversing. During the conversation, the Sufi used a word that could be interpreted as self-praise. After the conversation concluded, the Sufi reflected, "I hope I did not displease or anger Allah ﷻ. I don't care what this person thinks of me, but I do care if I offend Allah ﷻ."

IN PRACTICE

There is a high spiritual level that can be attained to do everything exclusively for Allah ﷻ. Although it is difficult to achieve this level in its purest form, it is always possible to strive for it and set it as a goal in one's actions and intentions. With Allah ﷻ's grace, one can hopefully attain this level of spiritual development.

Discussion Questions

- ► What are some of your spiritual goals?
- ► What are some ways to develop the habit of examining one's intentions?
- ► How does seeking to avoid displeasing Allah ﷻ contribute to developing integrity in one's interactions with the world?

101. Without Pain

One day, the Sufi pondered the wisdom of having nails that must be cut frequently. He reflected, "We could have been created without this necessity. There must be a rationale behind it." Then, while cutting his nails one day, he told himself, "If I cut any other part of my body, I will scream, but not my nails." Then he declared, "This is wisdom. If Allah ﷻ desires, He can create anything without pain in the body; however, everything is capable of becoming painful in the body!"

IN PRACTICE

It is crucial to recognize that Allah ﷻ is capable of anything beyond and in opposition to the laws of science. Occasionally, exceptions within a structure serve to remind us of this reality. Sometimes, we become so accustomed to routine procedures that we lose sight of the main objective and cannot see the big picture. In practice, it is essential to have this mindset of learning and deriving meaning from everything in relation to Allah ﷻ's original intent for its creation.

102. Achievements and Balance

The Sufi received word of an accomplishment she had earned one day. She was anticipating the results and had prepared herself so that she would not care if she received good news. The most essential aspect of her life was her relationship with Allah ﷻ. Nonetheless, as soon as she received the good news, something returned to her heart. She said to herself, "Over and over again! Even though I prepared myself beforehand, I cannot shake this revolting feeling of arrogance. Again, the agony of cleansing these emotions begins."

In practice

All spiritual or material accomplishments or victories can produce a bunch of losers. In other words, the points in life when we receive good news about our achievements, regardless of whether they are spiritual or worldly, can make a person arrogant with self-induced lies of pampering if they do not embody the truth that Allah ﷻ gives everything good. Therefore, all goodness and accomplishments are the result of the Mercy and Grace of Allah ﷻ bestowed upon the individual. Nevertheless, if the person still experiences these feelings, he or she must immediately engage in *astagfirullah,* or forgiveness, and *SubhanAllah wa bihamdihi,* or the remembrance of Allah ﷻ, in order to restore equilibrium and eliminate these false, reeking lies.

103. Best Husband Ever!

One day, the Sufi was out walking. He observed a man mowing and maintaining his lawn in front of his home. The man was wearing a shirt that read "Best Husband Ever!" The Sufi walked up to the man, smiled, and exclaimed, "Nice shirt!" Where did you purchase it?" The man exclaimed, "My wife purchased it for me!" Look at me! Don't you think I've earned it?

IN PRACTICE

It can be simple to make others happy. Especially in marital relationships, a minor issue can be a major issue for the other party. It is fascinating to examine Rasulullah's ﷺ familial relationships. Everyone was ecstatic about him. Rasulullah ﷺ was reportedly very relaxed with his family members in order to make them feel at ease. He was always cheerful, smiling and inquiring about the needs of others. Nonetheless, he took care of his own personal needs, such as sewing his clothes and cleaning, without seeking assistance from others.

Discussion Questions

- How do you make people happy? What thoughtful things do you say and do?
- What more things can you do, that you haven't already done, to make others happy?

104. Meeting After Years

There was a lamp that had been inoperable for years. The Sufi hoped that one day the lamp would function and emit light as it had in the past. The Sufi was reading the Qur'an and contemplating its meanings and possible interpretations one day. At that time, she needed more light to concentrate. She pressed the lamp's switch, and the lamp illuminated. The Sufi began to laugh and exclaimed, "You know when to work!"

IN PRACTICE

Everything is under the control of Allah ﷻ. In Sufi terms, the distinction between living and nonliving things can be deceiving. According to the teachings of the practice, so-called inanimate objects such as rocks and stones also glorify Allah ﷻ. Some individuals even hear their chants. In the preceding story, it is possible that the lamp did not want to miss the chance to give and share its light while the Sufi was studying the Noble Book of Allah ﷻ, the Qur'an.

Discussion Questions

- ▶ Have you ever had a friend arrive after many years of darkness and light up your life with the love of Allah ﷻ?

105. Thanking-Gratitude?

One day, the Sufi pondered how to remain humble when Allah ﷻ bestows constant blessings upon a person. Then she said, "Perhaps it is to express gratitude to Allah ﷻ with *Alhamdulillah.*" Then she said, "However, there are many people who may say Alhamdulillah but are still arrogant." Then, after some time, she said to herself, "True gratitude means understanding that these blessings are not the result of the person's virtue, but Allah ﷻ's."

IN PRACTICE

Alhamdulillah, which expresses gratitude to Allah ﷻ, is a difficult concept to embody. Simply stating the phrase is only the beginning. There is much work to be completed. Constant self-struggle against feelings of arrogance and showing gratitude toward Allah ﷻ can serve as two balancing factors in this conflict. Rasulullah was truly called and given the title "Muhammad" due to his embodiment of these teachings in his life, for which he truly expressed gratitude to Allah ﷻ.

106. Cat and the Sufi

The Sufi went home one day. The Sufi's husband was yelling at the cat to leave the house. The cat ran into the backyard. The husband began chasing the cat but was unsuccessful in capturing it. He then left. The Sufi was engaged in her duties at home. Then she noticed the cat. She attempted to capture the cat. She pondered, "What if I frighten the cat?" Then, she entered the backyard and began searching for the cat. The cat was gone. The Sufi searched for hours, but the cat was nowhere to be found. Typically, the cat never left the backyard. The Sufi felt terrible about the cat and prayed to Allah ﷻ for forgiveness.

IN PRACTICE

It is always possible to displease Allah ﷻ by breaking people's hearts or by oppressing a person or an animal. Therefore, a person should never take anything for granted or disregard any commitment, but should always be aware and vigilant. Sometimes a single word can strike fear into the hearts of others. Consequently, the individual may be punished after death.

107. Definition of Tea

Two friends, one from Egypt and the other from Turkey, visited a third friend from Egypt one day. The host asked, "What beverage would you like?" The Egyptian guest expressed gratitude by saying, "Thank you. Nothing ." The Turkish guest said, "I'll take some hot water poured over a tea bag." The Egyptian guest screamed and exclaimed, "That is what the Turkish call tea?!" The Turkish guest stated, "In Turkey, tea is prepared in a particular manner. Tea preparation requires at least 15 to 30 minutes."

IN PRACTICE

What we commonly refer to can have different meanings based on the individual, the culture, and the time period. Sometimes, a religious person may not be religious in the eyes of another. Similarly, the true value and meaning of all things are revealed when they are associated with Allah ﷻ. Thus, definitions are subject to change. Nonetheless, if one desires unchanging, permanent, or absolutes, he or she must connect themselves to Allah ﷻ, the One Who is Permanent.

108. Balash and Coffee in Egypt

An American was married to an Egyptian woman. After their wedding, they traveled to Egypt to see her family. The girl had relatives who owned a coffee shop in the same apartment building in which they formerly resided. After their arrival, the Egyptian wife suggested to her American husband, "Why don't you hang out with my cousins in the coffee shop while I visit my aunt on the second floor?" Because he enjoyed coffee so much, the husband was overjoyed. The cousins hugged the American husband of their relative and treated him with nice cappuccino. After he had finished, he was asked if he desired a second cup. The husband thought, "I might as well try something else." Then, he wanted mocha. After he drank, they politely inquired if he desired another. This lasted through the seventh cup. The exhausted Egyptian barista exclaimed, "*Balash*!" The husband comprehended the situation and said, "I truly value your hospitality."

IN PRACTICE

Everything is a *balash* from Allah ﷻ. *Balash* refers to something that is given without cost. Allah ﷻ provides so many things on a daily basis, including air, health, sight, hearing, digestion, and even excretion. Yet, we do not appear to recognize them and are ungrateful. Allah constantly bestows blessings upon mankind, despite the apparent simplicity of all these bounties.

Discussion Questions

- ▶ What are some ways you practice mindfulness in your daily life?
- ▶ What activity do you take time to slow down & really appreciate your day?
- ▶ How does practicing gratitude help your relationship with Allah ﷻ?

109. Harvard vs SubhanAllah

There once was a Sufi who attended Harvard. When she reunited with her friends during the winter break, everyone was talking about this Sufi and how she was attending such a prestigious institution. Each time they would say "Harvard," the Sufi would say "*Astagfirullah*" in her mind and heart. The Sufi then remarked to herself, "Every time they utter the word 'Harvard', it's as if they're dripping with satisfaction. "I wish they would say "*SubhanAllah*" for the essence of Allah's perfection in their hearts."

IN PRACTICE

It is essential to understand how we embody words. For instance, when a person says the word *Harvard*, if certain emotions arise in his or her mind and heart, this is a true embodiment, regardless of whether it is something right or wrong. Similarly, in spiritual endeavors, the full connection should exist when we say "*SubhanAllah*" to fill all of our body with the embodiment of 'perfection of Allah ﷻ; "*Alhamdulillah*" showing full and true gratitude only to Allah ﷻ; and "*Astagfirullah*" 'cleansing oneself from all the dirty and filthy feelings of arrogance and self-praise and asking Allah ﷻ for forgiveness for these false emotions. The Sufi wished that people's relationship with Allah ﷻ would be characterized by divine phrases, as opposed to phrases created by humans, such as *Harvard*. People admired the Sufi because she was a Harvard student, so she was reciting the phrase *Astagfirullah* in order to cleanse herself of any possible arrogance.

110. The Snake and Ungratefulness

The Sufi attended a gathering in the park one day. At the gathering, there were some impolite and disrespectful remarks about sacred objects, such as the divine Qur'an. The Sufi felt uneasy attending this gathering. As she was contemplating, she noticed a garden snake approaching her. The Sufi thought to herself, "This is a sign that I need to leave this gathering as soon as possible."

IN PRACTICE

One of a person's greatest assets is their relationship with Allah ﷻ through genuine *iman* or *tawhid*, which can be translated as the essence of genuine faith. In this instance, the individual is expected to be more overprotective of their *iman* than of their children or family members, wealth, and other assets. If the individual's *iman* is tainted, the value of the other things mentioned will also be tainted. When people have unthankful, disrespectful, and degrading attitudes toward Allahﷻ's sacred objects, one should leave the gathering, as the Sufi did, and even she received a sign to leave immediately.

Discussion Questions

▶ Have you ever found yourself in a situation where you became uncomfortable with the disrespectful behavior happening in the environment? How did it make you feel?

▶ How does that feeling compare with when you are in a gathering of people who respect each other and Allah ﷻ?

▶ Why do you think it makes a difference?

111. The True Reliance-*Tawakkul*

The Sufi thought to herself one day, "Whatever I asked, Allah ﷻ granted me from the apparent affairs of the world. I hope they will not bite me after death. Similar to the Prophet's prayers, I should now request whatever is good[x] in apparent worldly matters and continue to request the highest levels." Then, after some time, the Sufi began to experience unwelcome changes in her life. She continued to enjoy and appreciate the changes that Allah ﷻ bestowed upon her. She thought to herself one day, "Before, I used to ask, and Allah ﷻ granted my requests. Now, Allah ﷻ provides me with opportunities without my asking. I should always be pleased with Allah ﷻ regardless of the apparent evil or goodness of my destinies. I hope Allah ﷻ is pleased with me as well."

IN PRACTICE

The concept of reliance or *tawakkul* has varying degrees. One of the highest levels of this station is to dissolve one's own desires in Allah's ﷻ pleasure. This is comparable to the melting of a small ice cube in the ocean. In other words, when a person is pleased with Allah ﷻ in all encounters with apparent good and evil, it can be said that he or she is on the path of reliance, *tawakkul.* The expression *"I hope they don't come after death and bite me"* used by the Sufi in the preceding story alludes to the idea that we will be accountable to Allah ﷻ after death for the engagements in this life.

Discussion Questions

- ► Why is it so hard to give up self-will?
- ► How can I help myself to find the beautiful parts of bad-seeming things that happen in my life?
- ► How can I help myself to trust Allah ﷻ's will enough to surrender my will to Allah ﷻ's will in all my affairs?
- ► How would relying on Allah ﷻ entirely affect my relationship with Allah ﷻ?

112. The Professor & Four-Year Colleges

There was once a professor who was also a Sufi. One day, he reflected on his students. Every four years, new students would enroll while others would graduate. He thought to himself, "This is life precisely: freshman is the birth of the person; sophomore is the teenage & youth years; junior is the adulthood; and senior year is the old age; being ready to graduate and ready to die to meet with Allah ﷻ in order to face the outcome of all life efforts and to obtain the diploma."

IN PRACTICE

Life is in flux. A generation constantly and silently replaces the previous one. Each generation can be compared to college terms such as the class of 1976, 2019 or 2063, for instance. Even if a person desires to live a thousand years without dying, he or she should accept this temporal aspect of life.

113. Maintaining the Marriage

One day, the Sufi was giving his children advice. "Maintaining the marriage is the most difficult task," he stated. There are times when happiness comes naturally. There are also occasions when couples are upset. These are the times when you must avoid acting with ego, arrogance, and displays of power that communicate, "I don't need you." Humans are humans. Satan enjoys destroying the ties between people. Satan enjoys seeing broken families the most."

IN PRACTICE

As our emotions, spiritual states, and behaviors fluctuate with age, gender, culture, and different social dynamics, it is essential to first recognize this and then take preventative measures. It is a lie if one expects a marriage devoid of all problems. The reality is that such occurrences will occur, but the most important thing is to train ourselves to act positively and constructively with prudence in such circumstances. Current discourses center on events such as abuse, the legality of prenuptial agreements, and legal rights, among others. There are few or none spiritual trainings that emphasize wisdom in these marriages. There are few or none who provide genuine wisdom when advising married couples. The majority of advice assumes and discovers that the counseled is abused and oppressed, and as a result, they offer advice to combat, fight, and save the individual. It appears that the counseling language is devoid of these positive approaches.

114. Worms and their Purpose

One day, the Sufi placed the trash can by the side of the road. It was garbage day. While she was pulling the garbage can, a bag fell from the can onto the ground, followed by a large number of grain-sized worms. They were moving in every direction. The Sufi was extremely disgusted. She asked herself, "What is the wisdom behind their creation for spiritual journeys?"

IN PRACTICE

Any feelings of disgust can be attributed to a lack of appreciation and gratitude toward Allah ﷻ, the Creator. This is referred to in terminology as *kufr*. Any *kufr* actions can be compared to worms attacking one's *iman*, which is defined as one's sweet and honey-based appreciative and grateful relationship with Allah ﷻ. If a person has no *iman*, then he or she is susceptible to *kufr*. This person may not even be aware of these spiritual worms, as he or she is likely immersed in a swamp of worms.

Discussion Questions

▶ What is an important spiritual practice to do immediately when encountering feelings of disgust in order to start cleansing the heart?

115. The Man Being Fed with a Tube into his Body

The Sufi felt unwell one day and went to the mosque. Another Sufi saw him in the mosque and approached him, saying, "I just returned from visiting a friend. He is sick and at home. He cannot consume anything. They are feeding him through a tube that is connected to his stomach. His children are doctors and highly successful individuals. Yet they are unable to assist their father." The other Sufi then ceased speaking and left. The Sufi said to himself, "*Alhamdulillah,* thank you Allah ﷻ."

IN PRACTICE

We sometimes forget to be grateful to Allah, despite the fact that we may consider ourselves to be religious. Every instance of depressed feelings or emotions can be a sign of this ungrateful disposition toward Allah ﷻ. In the preceding narrative, when the other Sufi realized that his friend was experiencing an inner conflict, he rushed to his aid by recalling a personal experience. In practice, true friends assist one another, particularly when they are down and in need of spiritual support.

116. Time Travel

One day, the Sufi paid his friends a visit. A few people occupied a small room. Following their conversation, there was silence. The Sufi was engaged in computer work. He regarded the others. Everyone was either using a computer or a mobile phone. The Sufi stated, "If people from fifty years ago were to visit our era, they would find us strange."

IN PRACTICE

Change is desirable so long as it is beneficial and serves to strengthen one's relationship with Allah ﷻ. If it is the opposite, then the change is negative. One should ask Allah ﷻ for assistance and use one's willpower to avoid being swept away by distractions.

Discussion Questions

- ► How can I manage my screen time to help myself focus on my real life?
- ► In what ways has technology helped me as I continue to develop my relationship with Allah ﷻ?

117. The Intentions & the Relations with the Children

A Sufi used to make every effort to please her children. She treated them well so as not to be the "bad guy," but rather the "best friend." Another Sufi used to please Allah ﷻ and to treat her children accordingly. Unlike the previous Sufi, she was formerly a "bad guy" on occasion. After a few years, their children both grew up. The children who were treated well with the intention of pleasing them did not turn out to be more appreciative of their mother than the other children. The angry and mistreated mother asked herself, "What have I done wrong? I made every effort to satisfy them."

In practice

Before pleasing people, it is essential to have the intention to please Allah ﷻ. Allah can transform people's hearts, giving them love and appreciation for them. If this is done with this intention, then the same close friends or relationships can become a test or trial for us.

118. Adab the Core

One day, the Sufi was thinking about why Satan lost and angels won. Then, she said to herself, "It is the core, the *adab!*"

IN PRACTICE

Adab is the embodiment of having a positive opinion of Allah ﷻ at all times. People without *adab* may appear to be religious, but if they lack this understanding, this disease will eventually manifest. Satan is a perfect illustration of this. Angels are the antithesis. Humans are a mixture of angelic and demonic levels.

Satan lost *adab* by expressing displeasure with Allah ﷻ's Divine Will regarding the creation of humans. Angels maintained their *adab* by attempting to comprehend the wisdom behind the creation of humans and by submitting themselves completely to the Divine Will of Allah ﷻ. Both were tested on humans, and humans adapted by shifting between two extremes. Rasulullah possesses even greater submission to the Divine Will of Allah ﷺ than the angels. In contrast, humans exist at the lowest poles because they lack *adab*, but even they have surpassed Satan.

119. Heart & the Recognition

Recently, the Sufi avoided all social gatherings to prevent being recognized. The Sufi's husband pleaded and insisted that she accompany him to a social gathering one day. The Sufi accepted and said to herself, "I am aware that I will suffer in the future." She was present at the gathering. She attempted to monitor her heart rate. She realized that remnants of the desire to be acknowledged remained. The Sufi felt extremely uneasy with herself. After going to her place of seclusion, she created *istigfar*[18].

IN PRACTICE

It is crucial to continuously combat the heart's inherent diseases. One of these sicknesses is the desire of being acknowledged and praised by others. The ego desires titles, fame, and admiration from others. However, these can be spiritual filths comparable to, or perhaps worse than, urine and other impurities. The individual should constantly strive to transform their ego[19] into the content self[20].

---

18. asking forgiveness from Allah
19. Nafs-Ammarah, raw ego.
20. Nafs lawwamah (blaming self), nafs mutmainnah (satisfied self), and nafs radiyyah (fully pleased and happy self).

120. Fair Weather Friends

There were a number of dogs whose owners fed them delicious food every day. There was a dog named Kelb among them. All of the dogs, including Kelb, were very happy and proud of their owner. They held their master in the highest regard. After years of a pleasant, appreciative, and loyal relationship between the dogs and their owner, there were rumors that the owner was poisoning the dogs' food. All the dogs began discussing this rumor. A short time later, some of the dogs fed by their owner began to speak negatively about their owner. Kelb was shocked by this. The dogs began to abandon their owner. Several of them remained with their owner. Kelb thought to herself, "My friends' departure is disgraceful. "How can you be fed food for so many years and survive, only to abandon your owner because of rumors?"

IN PRACTICE

We gain knowledge from our teachers, who are also human. Even if our teachers make mistakes, we should have a more appreciation and loyalty toward them when they require our assistance. Even if they have never made a mistake, it has been common in the past and present for genuine educators to be the target of rumors and persecution.

One can observe the prime projection of this attitude between the person and Allah ﷻ. Allah ﷻ gives this person so much. One day, an unpleasant or evil-seeming incident touches this person. Then, this person stops his or her relationship with Allah ﷻ. What a loss on the person's part!

ENDNOTES

<ol style="list-style-type: lower-roman">
<li>[49:2–4]</li>
<li>[49:13]</li>
<li>[39, 42]</li>
<li>[41, 21]</li>
<li>[49:2]</li>
<li>[94:1–8]</li>
<li>[3,159]</li>
<li>Called "sir" in terminology.</li>
<li>Sunnah or masnun duas.</li>
<li>khayr</li>
</ol>

BIBLIOGRAPHY

[1] Al-Ghazzali, M. *Al-Ghazzali on Knowing Yourself and Allah* ﷾. Kazi Publications Inc., 2003.

[2] Vahide, S. *The Collection of Light.* ihlas nur publication, 2001.

[3] al-Ba'uniyyah, A. *The Principles of Sufism.* NYU Press, 2016.

[4] Kumek, Y. J. *Practical Mysticism: Sufi Journeys of Heart and Mind.* Kendall Hunt, 2018.

[5] Muslim, A. *Sahih Muslim,* translated by A. Siddiqui. Peace Vision. 1972.

[6] Al-Bukhari, M. *The Translation of the Meanings of Sahih Al-Bukhari.* Kazi Publications, 1986.

[7] Ozkan, T. Y. *A Muslim Response to Evil: S. N. on the Theodicy.* Routledge, 2016.

[8] Murad, K. *In The Early Hours: Reflections on Spiritual and Self Development.* Kube Publishing Ltd, 2013.

[9] U. P. Oxford, "Oxford Dictionaries," 2016, http://www.oxforddictionaries.com/us/definition/american_english/.

[10] Al-Ghazali, M. *Deliverance from Error.* Louisville: Fons Vitae, 2000.

[11] Ali, A. Y. *The Meaning of the Glorious Qurān.* Islamic Books, 1938.

[12] Dawud, A. *Sunan Abu Dawud.* Darussalam, 2008.

[13] Ashraf, M. M. K. 'Alī Thānvī, *The Path to Perfection: An Edited Anthology of the Spiritual Teachings of Hakīm Al-Umma Mawlānā Ashraf 'Alī Thānawī.* White Thread, 2005.

[14] Ibn Qayyim. I. K. *The Soul's Journey After Death.* Noah, 2018.

[15] Vandestra, M. *Human Souls Journey After Death In Islam.* Dragon Promedia, 2017.

[16] Hanbal, A. B. *Musnad Imam Ahmad Ibn Hanbal.* Dar-Us-Salam Publications, 2012.

[17] U. P. Oxford, "Oxford Dictionaries," 2016. [Online]. Available: http://www.oxforddictionaries.com/us/definition/american_english/.

[18] Al-Ghazali, M. *Deliverance from Error,* Louisville: Fons Vitae, 2000.

[19] Salamah-Qudsi, A. *Sufism and Early Islamic Piety: Personal and Communal Dynamics.* Cambridge University Press, 2018.

[20] Muslim, A. *Sahih Muslim* (translated by Siddiqui, A.). Peace Vision. 1972.

[21] Hanbal, A. B. *Musnad Imam Ahmad Ibn Hanbal.* Dar-Us-Salam Publications, 2012.

[22] Kumek, Y. J. *Practical Mysticism: Sufi Journeys of Heart and Mind.* Kendall Hunt, 2018.

[23] Ansar, A. *Peace of Mind and Healing Broken Lives.* Universal Mercy, 2010.

[24] Smith, J. I. and Y. Y. Haddad. *The Islamic Understanding of Death and Resurrection.* Oxford University Press, 2002.

[25] Dorothy, G. and J. L. Singer. *Handbook of Children and the Media.* SAGE, 2002.

[26] Ring, N.C. *Introduction to the Study of Religion.* New York: Orbis, 2007.

[27] Ozkan, T. Y. *A Muslim Response to Evil: S. N. on the Theodicy.* Routledge, 2016.

[28] Al-Bukhari, M. *The Translation of the Meanings of Sahih Al-Bukhari.* Kazi Publications, 1986.

[29] Al-Ansari, A. B. "Ahadith al-Shuyukh al-Thiqat," vol. 2, no. 322, pp. 875–876.

[30] Tamer, Georges. *Islam and Rationality: The Impact of Al-Ghazālī: Papers Collected on His 900th Anniversary.* Boston: BRILL, 2015.

[31] Geoffroy, Eric, and Roger Gaetani. *Introduction to Sufism: The Inner Path of Islam.* Bloomington, Ind: World Wisdom, 2010.

[32] Shah, Idries. *The Sufis.* London: The Octagon Press, 1999.

[33] Jamal, Azim, and Nido R. Qubein. *Life Balance: The Sufi Way.* Mumbai, India: Jaico Pub. House, 2000.

[34] Shah, I. *Learning How to Learn: Psychology and Spirituality in the Sufi Way.* Octagon Press Ltd., 1978.

[35] Heer, Nicholas, Kenneth L. Honerkamp, al-Tirmidhī M. A. Hakīm, Muhammad -H. Sulamī, and Muhammad -H. Sulamī. *Three Early Sufi Texts.* Louisville: Fons Vitae, 2009.

[36] Singh, David E. *Sainthood and Revelatory Discourse: An Examination of the Bases for the Authority of Bayan in Mahwi Islam.* Delhi: Regnum International, 2003.

[37] Darimi, I. *Sunan Darimi.* Dar Al Kitab, 1997.

[38] Bukhari, M.I. I. *Moral Teachings of Islam: Prophetic Traditions from Al-Adab Al-mufrad.* Rowman Altamira, 2003.

[39] Schimmel, Annemarie, and Friedrich Heiler. *Deciphering the Signs of Allah ﷺ: A Phenomenological Approach to Islam ; [to the Memory of Friedrich Heiler (1892–1967)].* Albany: State Uni. of New York Press, 1994.

[40] Stowasser, Barbara F. *The Day Begins at Sunset: Perceptions of Time in the Islamic World.* I.B.Tauris, 2014.

[41] Al-Qahtani, S. B. W. *Fortress Of Muslim.* Darussalam Publishers, 2018.

[42] Abū, Dā'ūd S.-A.-S, and Ahmad Hasan. *Sunan Abu Dawud.* New Delhi: Kitab Bhavan, 2012.

[43] al-Qushayri, Abu -Q, and Alexander D. Knysh. *Al-qushayri's Epistle on Sufism: Al-risala Al-Qushayriyya Fi 'ilm Al-Tasawwuf.* Reading: Garnet Publishing, 2007.

[44] Ibn Qayyim, I. K. *The Soul's Journey After Death.* Noah, 2018.

[45] Khan, M. A. *Encyclopaedia of Sufism: Sufism and Naqshbandi order.* Anmol Publications, 2003.

[46] Adonis. *Sufism and Surrealism.* Saqi, 2013.

[47] Muhaiyaddeen, M R. B. *Dhikr: The Remembrance of Allah ﷺ.* Narbeth, Pa: Fellowship Press, 1999.

[48] Abdullah, P. M. *ISLAMIC TASAWWUF: Shariah And Tariqah.* Adam Publishers & Distributors, 2001.

[49] Vaughan-Lee, Llewellyn. *Love is a Fire: The Sufi's Mystical Journey Home.* The Golden Sufi Center, 2000.

[50] I. Majah, *Sunan Ibn Majah,* Kazi Publications, 1993.

[51] A. R. A. Nisa, *Sunan Nisai,* Kazi Publications, 1997.

[52] A. Muslim, Sahih Muslim (translated by Siddiqui, A.), *Peace Vision,* 1972.

[53] M. Tirmizi, Jami At-Tirmizi, *Dar-us-Salam,* 2007.

[54] M. Al-Bukhari, *The translation of the meanings of Sahih Al-Bukhari,* Kazi Publications, 1986.

[55] M. i. `. A. K. Al-Tabrizi, Mishkat al Masabih, Beirut: Dar Ibn Hazm, 2003.

[56] SInternational, *The Qurān,* Abul-Qasim Publishing House, 1997.

[57] S. Abu-Dawud, Sunan Abu Dawud, *Riyadh: Darussalam,* 2008.

GLOSSARY

A'bd: worshipper, servant, or slave

Accountability: liability, especially in Sufism and in Abrahamic traditions, everyone has a free will or agency in this world but accountability for their actions in the afterlife in front of Allah ﷻ

Adab: good manners, esp. in the relationship with Allah ﷻ in Sufism

Adjective: attribute, a phrase describing a noun

Adonai: name of Allah ﷻ in Judaism

Affair: relationship

Agency: acting as an agent or a carrier with free will

Alhamdulillah: a chanted divine phrase of appreciation of Allah ﷻ or Allah

Alienating: isolating, separating, disconnecting

Alienating Images of Allah ﷻ: understandings about Allah ﷻ that disconnects person to establish a regular relationship with the Divine or to follow a religion

Allah (ﷻ): Allah سبحانه وتعالى. The expression سبحانه وتعالى read as Subhānahu wa Tā'la also abbreviated as SWT and written as also Allah (SWT) is an expression of respect when the Name of Allah is mentioned. Among these expressions many English translations, one can be "Allah is One, Unique and Perfect with all the Divine Attributes and Names, far beyond human's negative and wrong constructions and imaginations. All Glory Belongs to Allah, the Most Exalted, the Most Respected, and the Most High."

Allude: explain, refer

Anger: uncontrolled and chaotic human spiritual state

Aphorism: sayings, proverbs in a culture, society, or belief

Appreciate: thank

Appreciative: with capital A, Allah ﷻ

Arabic: language, especially the language of revelation of the Qurãn

Arrogance: feelings and actions of superiority

Ascension: rising, especially in Sufism increase of spiritual states in relationship with Allah ﷻ

Assert: claim

Astagfirullah: a divine phrase of asking forgiveness from Allah ﷻ and cleaning the heart

Attribute: adjective, a phrase describing a noun, especially in Sufism, attributes of Allah ﷻ: divine phrases describing Allah ﷻ

Authentic: original, genuine, true

Balance: modesty, especially in Sufism, following the middle way

Behavior: temporary nature of a person

Bismillah: a divine phrase of starting something with the blessing of Allah ﷻ

Book of Chant: the Qurãn

Boost: increase

Bowing down: bending one's body, especially the act of respect by bending one's body, for Allah ﷻ

Candy: hard delight, especially in Sufism, the pleasures or miracles given to the person on the path of Allah ﷻ

Caution: carefulness, alertness, especially in Sufism, in spiritual manners not to be trapped by ego or self

Certainty: knowing without doubt, especially in Sufism, knowing and experiencing without doubt

Chanting: repeating, especially in Sufism, repeating the phrases with focus and experience

Chaos: disorder and confusion, especially in Sufism (spiritual) chaos being in negative states of anxiety, stress, and purposelessness

Charge: positive states of spirituality that makes the person happy, peaceful, and calm, especially in Sufism, filling oneself with divine knowledge and experience

Compassion: loving and caring

Confirming Book: the Qurãn

Confirming Scripture: the Qurãn

Conscience: internal instinct of distinguishing right or wrong

Consciousness: awareness

Constant: not changing, permanent, especially in practice, known as Reflective Attributes of Allah ﷻ, where humans have an image but Allah ﷻ has its source

Construction: formation of an abstract entity

Contract: squeeze

Convergence: similarity

Cookie: soft delight, small sweet cake, especially in Sufism, the pleasures or miracles given to the person on the path of Allah ﷻ

Cosmology: knowledge about the origin and development of the universe

Covenant: agreement

Death: end of physical faculties of a person, especially physical versus spiritual death; the soul does not die but the body dies in understanding of physical death in Islam

Dedication: sincere constant effort

Deity: representation of the transcendent

Detox: discharge

Devout: pious, practicing

Dhikr: as one of the names of the Qurãn, or any type of chant to remember Allah ﷻ

Discharge: negative states of spirituality that makes the person sad, stressed, and anxious, especially in Sufism, emptying oneself from all the temporal and worldly positive and negative attachments

Divine: transcendent

Doctrine: teaching

Dominance: control

Dream: visions when one is sleeping or awake

Ego: self, identifier of a person, especially in Sufism, raw and uneducated identifier and controller of a person

Elohim: name of Allah ﷻ in Judaism

Embodiment, versus embody: making it part of one's character

Endeavor: engagement, activities

Epistemology: theory of knowledge

Ethical: moral

Ethnographic: based on observation

Etiquette: good manners and respect, especially in Sufism, respect in the relationship with Allah ﷻ

Evil: anything that causes stress, sadness, or anxiety

Evil eye: the belief of unknown effects of the human eye across different cultures, traditions, and religions, especially in Sufism the evil eye effects due to extreme hatred, jealousy, or, oppositely, evil eye effects due to extreme veneration and love of someone

Expand: enlarge

Experience: internalization of knowledge

Experience or experiential knowledge: all types of learning except from a book or a teacher, internalizing and personalizing the formal learning

Figurative: unclear, secondary, and metaphorical

Free Will: free choice of a person in decision-making

Generous: with capital G, Allah ﷻ

Genre: type

Genuine: sincere, original, authentic

Ghazali: philosopher, theologician, Sufi mystic, lived in 12th century

Glorification: the mental, spiritual, and maybe verbal act of describing Allah ﷻ in an admirable way

Groundless: fake

Habitual: habit of doing something constantly

HasbiyaAllah: a chant with a meaning of "Allah ﷻ is sufficient for me"

Healthy Cookies: beneficial extraordinary incidents, such as miracles in Sufism

Heaven: a place of all maximized pleasures of bodily and spiritual engagements while being with Allah ﷻ

Hell: a place of punishment

Heretic: abnormal person, especially in Sufism, a desired state of being to experience and know the Divine

Humbleness: behavior of modesty in viewing oneself, especially in Sufism, accepting the weakness in one's relationship with Allah ﷻ and not being disrespectful and arrogant to Allah ﷻ

Humility: character or trait of humbleness

Illa Allah: "except Allah" or "except Allah ﷻ"

Images of Allah ﷻ: understandings and experiences about Allah ﷻ

Imitation: trying without real understanding

Infinite: Allah ﷻ, the Unlimited

Informant: a person who participates in anthropological research

InshAllah: Allah ﷻ willing, hopefully

Intention: planning ideas before the action

Internalize: making it part of one's character, trait, or nature in Sufism

Intrinsic: internal

Islam: name of a religion that emphasizes believing in one Allah ﷻ and Jesus, Moses, and Muhammad to be the human prophets of the Creator

Jihad: struggle, esp. spiritual struggle within oneself

Joseph: Prophet of Allah ﷻ in Islam, Christianity, and Judaism

Journey: struggles of following guidelines of a mystical school

Khidr: mystical being who is sent by Allah ﷻ at any time to help people in their problems; also believed to be the teacher of Moses in a mystical journey as mentioned in the Qurãn

Kitab: the Qurãn

Knowledge: theoretical understanding of something through education

La ilaha illa Allah: there is no Allah ﷻ except Allah, a critical Divine phrase of chanting in Sufism implying a spiritual charge and discharge

Literal: clear and primary

Lord: Allah ﷻ

Lucifer: Satan, mentioned in divine Qurãn such as the Bible and the Qurãn

Majnun: crazy or, especially in Sufism, heretic

Mantra: a repetitive phrase or sound, especially used in Hinduism and Buddhism

Meditation: deep focus especially with reflection

Memorization: learning by heart

Mercy: compassion and forgiveness

Middle way: living a balanced life in spiritual and worldly engagements

Mimic: imitate

Mind: logic, reason, and rationality

Miracle: incidents against the law of physics and against all natural sciences

Mosque: temple of Muslims

Muhammad: Rasulullah ﷺ of Islam, referred as "the Prophet" in the text

Musaddiq: the Qurān

Mystic: a person who adopts the teachings of mysticism

Mysticism: the knowledge of the transcendent

Nafs: self in its raw form

Neat: tidy and in order

Negation: denial, esp. in Sufism, emptying from the mind and heart the imperfect ideas and feelings about Allah ﷻ

Neglectful: not giving the proper attention that is due

Notion: concept, idea

Ocean: a very large sea, especially in Sufism, represents Allah ﷻ the Unlimited or Allah ﷻ's Unlimited and Incomprehensible Knowledge

Odd: not even, unique, no equivalence

Olam: hidden, waiting to be discovered through experiential knowledge

One: with capital denoting the one and only Creator

Oppression: unjust action of the strong over the weak

Permanent: constant, not changing, not ending

Phenomenon: occurrence

Pious: devout, practicing

Poisonous Cookies: harmful extraordinary incidents, such as miracles in Sufism

Pollution: making something dirty

Popular culture: the ethnographic data gathered over the period of years among different Sufi communities

Preposition: a word that does not have a meaning by itself but has a meaning in relation to another word, especially in Sufism, prepositions having conceptual and terminological meanings when one describes the relationships with the Divine

Pronunciation: correct sounds of letters in a language

The Prophet: Rasulullah ﷺ *Muhammad (peace and blessings be upon him). The Arabic writing* ﷺ is read as "Sallahu alayhi wa salllam" abbreviated as "saws" when the name of Rasulullah ﷺ Muhammad is mentioned. The expressions ﷺ or saws are expressions and phrases of blessings and peace for Rasulullah ﷺ Muhammad. They are also the expressions and phrases of blessings and peace used for the other Prophets of Allah such as Abraham, Moses, and Jesus and others.

Prostration versus to prostrate: the act of respect by putting one's face on the ground, especially in Sufism, humbling oneself for Allah ﷻ by putting the face, the noble part of the body, on the ground

Qibla: the direction where Muslims and Sufis turn when they pray

Qurãn: sacred text of Muslims

Rabbinic: related with the Rabbis, the priests, and teachers of Judaism Recitation, versus to recite: reading versus to read

Rasulullah ﷺ**:** The word Rasulullah can be translated as "the Messenger or Prophet of Allah." Rasulullah in its usage is Rasulullah ﷺ *Muhammad (peace and blessings be upon him)* (PBUH). PBUH: *Peace and blessings be upon Him*

Reliance: dependence

Repetition: repeating

Reverence: respect

Reward: prize, payment, especially in worldly and afterlife rewards in Islam

Ritual: practices in a religion or mysticism that have spiritual and divine value for a person

Ruku: bowing down

Rumi: great Sufi mystic

Saint: the person believed to be close to Allah ﷻ

Sakina: peaceful and calm feelings

Salawat: names of the chants to remember teachers and their covenants with their students, especially the main teacher, Rasulullah ﷺ Muhammad and others, such as Abraham, Moses, and Jesus

Samad: the One who does not need anything, but everyone and everything needs Allah ﷻ

Satan: the Devil, Lucifer, mentioned in divine Qurãn such as in the Bible and the Qurãn

SAW: "Sallahu alayhi wa salllam" abbreviated as "saws" when the name of Rasulullah ﷺ Muhammad is mentioned. The expressions ﷺ or saws are expressions and phrases of blessings and peace for Rasulullah ﷺ Muhammad and other prophets such as Abraham, Moses, Jesus and others.

Scent: perfume, nice smell

Scholar: expert, especially in Sufism, the experts who practice what they teach (alim)

Scripture: sacred book or sacred text

Self: ego, identifier of a person, especially in Sufism, raw and uneducated identifier and controller of a person

Service: ethical action of doing good for others and society

Spiritual Journey: struggles of following guidelines of a mystical school

State: level, especially in Sufism, spiritual level

Struggle: efforts to achieve a goal

SubhanAllah: glorification of Allah ﷻ, a divine phrase of chanting of spirituality implying a spiritual charge and discharge

SubhanAllahu wa bihamdihi: a divine phrase of glorification of Allah ﷻ

SubhanAllahul Azeem: a divine phrase of glorification of Allah ﷻ in the prostration posture

SubhanRabbiyalAzim: phrase of glorification for Allah ﷻ in the bowing posture

Submission: natural acceptance of the uncontrolled and unseen

Sufi: follower of Sufism

Sufism: mystical path of Islam

Superstitious: fake

Surrender: involuntary state of acceptance of the uncontrolled and the unseen

SWT: Subhānahu wa Tā'la also abbreviated as SWT and written as also Allah (ﷻ) is an expression of respect when the Name of Allah is mentioned.

Tahajjud: night prayer

Talismanic: unknown and indescribable effects of divine words and sounds

Taqwa: respect of Allah ﷻ

Taste: pleasure, especially spiritual pleasure such as peace, calmness, joy, and happiness in Sufism

Temple: worship place

Temporal: ending

Temporary: transitory

Temptation: false ideas

The Curer: Allah ﷻ

The Divine: Allah ﷻ

The Forgiver: a name of Allah ﷻ in Sufism

The Friend: a name of Allah ﷻ in Sufism

The Helper: a name of Allah ﷻ in Sufism

The Lover: a name of Allah ﷻ in Sufism

The Peace Giver: Allah ﷻ

The Prophet: Muhammad, Rasulullah ﷺ of Islam, referred as "the Prophet" in the text

The Real: Allah ﷻ

The Real Maker: Allah ﷻ

The Source: Allah ﷻ

The Sustainer: a name of Allah ﷻ in Sufism

The Reminder: the Qurãn

The Wise: with capital W, Allah ﷻ

Throne: a figurative or metaphorical representation of dominion of Allah ﷻ

Trait: permanent character or nature

Tranquility: peace and calmness

Transcendent: beyond human limits

Transitory: temporal

Transliteration: writing the sounds of words or phrases in one language with an alphabet of another language

Union: being together, especially in this book, goal and joy of being always in the presence of Allah ﷻ

Unseen: anything five senses cannot testify in scientific methods

Weak: not having a physical strength to perform an action, especially in Sufism, not having spiritual strength to perform any action

Worshipper: a person who regularly follows and practices rituals, acts of prayers

ACKNOWLEDGMENTS

I would like to thank all my unnamed teachers, friends, and students for their input, ideas, suggestions, help, and support during and before the preparation of this book.

I would like to thank Dr. David Banks, faculty of the Department of Anthropology, State University of New York (SUNY), Sister Toni Hajdaj, Sister Umm Aisha, Dr. AbdulAhad, Br. Ali Rifat and His wife Sister Yildiz at-Turki, Sheikh Dr. Omar of Maryland al-Hindi, Sheikh Tamer of Buffalo, and Sheikh Ali of Hartford Seminary, Sisters Asya Hamad, Amina Osman, and Fatima Samrodia of Darul-Ulum Madania of Buffalo for all their editing, suggestions and comments.

I want to also thank the team of Medina House Publishing in all their preparations and efforts at all stages of this book especially Br. Murat, Br. Khalid (Halit), Br. Mehmet (Matt), Sister Karen, Sister Dorothy-Damla, and Sister Anna Engle.

Lastly, I would like to thank all of my family members for their patience with me during the preparation of this book.

We ask Allah ﷻ to accept all our efforts with the Divine Karam, Fadl, and Grace but not with our faulty and limited efforts deeming rejection. اللَّهُمَّ صلِّ عَلى سَيِّدِناَ وَ حَبِيْبَنَا وَ مَوْلَاناَ مُحَمَّد.

AUTHOR BIO

Dr. M. Yunus Kumek is currently teaching on Muslim Ministry and Spiritual Care at Harvard Divinity School. He has been religious studies coordinator at State University of New York (SUNY) Buffalo State and teaching undergraduate and graduate courses in religious studies at SUNY at Buffalo State, Niagara University and Daemen College. Before becoming interested in religious studies, Dr. Kumek was doing his doctorate degree in physics at SUNY at Buffalo, and had published academic papers in the areas of quantum physics and medical physics. Then, he decided to engage with the world of social sciences through social anthropology, education, and cultural anthropology in his doctorate studies and subsequently, spent a few years as a research associate in the anthropology department of the same university. Recently, he completed a postdoctoral fellowship at Harvard Divinity school and published books on religious literacy through ethnography and selected passages from the Quran with interpreted contextual meanings. Dr. Kumek had classical training in Islamic sciences from the teachers of Egypt, India, Turkey, Yemen, Somalia, Morocco, and the United States. He stayed and studied in Egypt and Turkey. Dr. Kumek, who remains interested in physics—solves physics problems to relax—enjoys different languages: German, Spanish, Arabic, Urdu, and Turkish, especially in his research of scriptural analysis. Dr. Kumek takes great pleasure in classical poetry as well.

SUGGESTED READINGS

Al-Ghazali, M. *Deliverance from Error*. Fons Vitae, 2000.

Al-Ghazali, M. *Ihya 'Ulum al-Din.'* Dar al-Fikr, 2004.

Al-Ghazzali, M. *On the Treatment of Anger, Hatred and Envy*. Kazi Publications, 2003.

Al-Ghazzali, M. *The Alchemy of Happiness*. Routledge, 2015.

Ali, A. Y. *The Meaning of the Glorious Qurãn*. Islamic Books, 1938.

Anjum, Z. Iqbal: *The Life of a Poet, Philosopher, and Politician*. Random House, 2015.

Arberry, A. *Interpretation of Koran*. Macmillan, 1955.

Arberry. *Muslim Saints and Mystics: Episodes from Tadhirat al awliya of Faird al-Din Attar, Omphaloskepsis*, 2000.

Asad, M. *The Message of the Qurãn: Translated and Explained*. Al-Andalus Gibraltar, 1980.

Avery, K. S. *A Psychology of Early Sufi Sama: Listening and Altered States*. Routledge, 2004.

Awang, R. "Anger Management: A Psychotherapy Sufistic Approach," vol. 9, no. 1, 2014, pp. 13–15.

Barks, C. *Rumi: Bridge to the Soul*. Harperone, 2007.

Barks, R. N. C. with J. Moyne, Rumi, Jelaluddin. "The guest house." *The Essential Rumi*. Harper, 1995, p. 109.

Bayrak, T. *The Name & the Named*. Canada, 2000.

Berguno, G. & Loutfy, N. "The Existential Thoughts of the Sufis. Existential Analysis." *Journal of the Society for Existential Analysis*, vol. 16, no. 1, 2005.

Bowen, J. *A New Anthropology of Islam*. Cambridge University Press, 2012.

Clarke, M. "Cough Sweets and Angels: The Ordinary Ethics of the Extraordinary in Sufi Practice in Lebanon." *Journal of the Royal Anthropological Institute*, vol. 20, no. 3, 2014, pp. 407–25.

Cutsinger, J. S. *Paths to the Heart.* World Wisdom, 2010.

Douglas-Klotz, N. *The Sufi Book of Life: 99 Pathways of the Heart for the Modern Dervish.* Penguin, 2005.

Ernst, C. W. *Teachings of Sufism.* Shambhala Publications, 1999.

Esposito, J. *The Oxford Dictionary of Islam.* Oxford University Press, 2014.

Friedlander, S. *The Whirling Dervishes: Being an Account of the Sufi Order Known as the Mevlevis and its Founder the Poet and Mystic Mevlana Jalalu'ddin Rumi.* SUNY Press, 1975.

Geoffroy, E. *Introduction to Sufism: The Inner Path of Islam.* World Wisdom, Inc., 2010.

Gibran, K. *The Prophet.* Oneworld Publications, 2012.

Hanson, Y. H. "The Creed of Imam Al-Tahawi." Zaytuna Institute, California, 2007.

Hanson, Y. H. *Purification of the Heart.* Alhambra Productions, 1998.

Helminski, K. *The Knowing Heart: A Sufi Path of Transformation.* Shambhala Publications, 2000.

Izutsu, T. *Sufism and Taoism: A Comparative Study of Key Philosophical Concepts.* University of California Press, 2016.

James, W. "The Will to Believe." *New World,* 1896.

Jawziyyah, Q. *The Prophetic Medical Science.* Idara Impex, 2013.

Karamustafa, T. A. *Sufism.* Edinburgh University Press, 2007.

Katz, J. G. "Dreams, Sufism, and Sainthood." *Brill,* vol. 71, 1996.

Khan, Z. M. *Gardens of the Righteous.* Routledge, 2012.

Lewis, B. *Music of a Distant Drum: Classical Arabic, Persian, Turkish, and Hebrew Poems.* Princeton University Press, 2001.

Malak, A. *Muslim Narratives and the Discourse of English.* SUNY Press, 2007.

Morris, J. W. "Introducing Ibn 'Arabī's Book of Spiritual Advice." *Journal of the Muhyiddīn Ibn 'Arabī Society,* no. 28, 2000, pp. 1–17.

Pickthall, M. W. E. *Holy Qurān.* Kutub Khana Isha'at-ul-Islam, 1977.

Ramji, R. *The Global Migration of Sufi Islam to South Asia and Beyond.* Brill, 2007, pp. 473–84.

Renard J. *Knowledge of Allah ﷺ in Classical Sufism: Foundations of Islamic Mystical Theology.* Paulist Press, 2004.

Rumi, J. *The Essential Rumi.* Harper, 1996.

Schimmel, A. *Deciphering the Signs of Allah ﷻ: A Phenomenological Approach to Islam.* State University of New York Press, 1994.

Siddiqui, A. "Sahih Muslim." *Peace Vision,* 1972.

Trimingham, J. S. *The Sufi Orders in Islam.* Oxford University Press, 1998.

Upton, C. *Doorkeeper of the Heart: Versions of Rabi'a.* Threshold Books, 1988.

Usmani, T. *An Approach to the Qur'anic Sciences.* Adam Publishers, 2006.

INDEX